Bloom!

What People Are Saying About
Cecilia Carter and *Bloom!*

"It's one thing to know CeCe as my first cousin, who, practically speaking, is the sister I never wanted or asked for—one who got better grades and was infinitely more popular throughout our formative years. However, pride has long replaced jealousy, especially as I read *Bloom!* by Cecilia Carter. The smart girl I once knew has evolved into a brilliant strategist, employing complex methods like vision-setting and scenario planning to coach us. While her focus primarily targets women, men can benefit too as we navigate today's challenges and struggles on the path to self-discovery and empowerment.

Bloom! confirms what I suspected years ago—that CeCe would become The Strategy Chick and be one helluva coach!"

– Michael Wilbon, American Commentator and former sportswriter and columnist for The Washington Post

"*Bloom!* is the truth we needed to hear in 2024 and beyond. It's a collection of short stories and anecdotes from throughout Cecilia's career —all real, all relatable, and all applicable to the learning we each must go through to live our most meaningful and purpose-driven lives. There are coaching exercises, tools, and —most wonderfully, for me—'Golden Eggs' that help distill each chapter's lessons learned for maximum improvement and self-reflection. My girl CeCe has gone from an amazing colleague I was happy to see in my office every day to a world-class purveyor of knowledge and wisdom at scale. I had the benefit of the Strategy Chick's counsel at close range for years and now readers around the world have the key to unlock those same secrets at their fingertips with *Bloom!*"

— **Corey duBrowa**, CEO Burson

"Bloom! does just that…it guides the reader through self-reflection and discovery, allowing one to blossom from Cece's personal and professional journey. Powerful, yet practical, *Bloom!* reveals the brilliance of the Strategy Chick's coaching."

— **Candace Matthews**, Board Director/Retired Corporate Executive

"Bloom! is the inspiring call to action we all need to reclaim our power and live life on our own terms. Cecilia masterfully weaves her engaging style and profound wisdom into each story and strategy, guiding you on your journey of self-empowerment. Get ready to embrace your potential and blossom!"

— **Dr. Charlotte Jones-Burton**, Biopharmaceutical Executive, Investor and Board of Director

"Bloom! is a powerful journey that reminds us that growth is a process, working through fear can be our single greatest opportunity, and resilience demands real work. Cecilia's courage, candor, and wisdom are distilled in these pages, making this book both a practical guide and a profound call to action for anyone ready to step into their power to be their very best selves and shape a better future for others."

— **Jonathan Kirschner**, CEO of AIIR Consulting

"Cecilia Carter was invaluable in helping me understand how to deliver impact as my authentic self. *Bloom!* expands her reach allowing many more people to access the tools and strategies to help them through their self-empowerment journeys."
— **Kathy Fernando**, Ph.D., Senior Vice President and Global Head of Pfizer Ignite

"*Bloom!* is an inspiring and practical guide that invites you to step into your power and rediscover the strength that's been within you all along. Through heartfelt stories of everyday people rising to extraordinary heights, this book will awaken your courage, ignite your confidence, and transform the way you move through your life and career. A must-read for anyone ready to embrace their true potential and create a future filled with purpose, passion, and possibility."
— **Amy Kavanaugh Mason**, Co-founder, Candified

"Cecilia Carter is an exceptional executive coach who has a significant impact on both professional and personal growth. With her vast experience and deep commitment to leadership development, Cecilia has a profound ability to unlock potential in a way that's both transformative and empowering. Her unique blend of intelligence, passion, and humor pushes clients beyond their comfort zones, inspiring them to lead authentically and confidently. Whether you're an emerging leader or a seasoned executive, working with Cecilia provides lasting clarity, growth, and inspiration, making her an invaluable guide on any leadership journey."
— **Liana Gordon Kahn**, Director of Executive Coaching & Development, Keystone Partners

"*Bloom!* reminds us there is something within each of us—a potential—that, when properly nurtured and cared for, can grow and flourish into something beautiful and powerful. Just like a flower needs the right conditions to thrive, we too can reach our fullest potential when given the right support and nourishment."

– Derek Phillips, Founder, Executive Director
Real Dads Network

Bloom!

The Strategy Chick's Guide to
UNLOCKING YOUR POWER

CECILIA CARTER

"The Strategy Chick®"

Publishing support provided by
Ignite Press
55 Shaw Ave. Suite 204
Clovis, CA 93612
www.IgnitePress.us

ISBN: 979-8-9924161-0-7
ISBN: 979-8-9924161-1-4 (E-book)
ISBN: 979-8-9924161-2-1 (Hardcover)

For bulk purchases and for booking, contact:

Cecilia Carter
The Strategy Chick®
Cecilia@thestrategychick.com
www.thestrategychick.com

Library of Congress Control Number: 2025900319

Cover design by Usman Tariq
Edited by Zoe Herald
Interior design by Jetlaunch

FIRST EDITION

I dedicate this book to all women, but especially to my daughters, Chandler and Camdyn. You are navigating your journeys of living authentically, pushing aside insecurities, and defining your brand in a challenging world. May this book be a source of inspiration and a reminder that your voices are powerful, your talents are mighty, and you will bloom.

TABLE OF CONTENTS

INTRODUCTION

Do you feel as though your life is at a standstill, watching others flourish while you wait for your own season to bloom? You've invested in yourself, built your skills, career, and relationships, but still feel blocked by setbacks, doubts, or barriers. When you add the challenges of feeling marginalized, misunderstood, or even held back by expectations, it's easy to see how seeds of doubt can grow in place of the vibrant landscape you've envisioned.

How can you overcome your fears, regain your confidence and claim the life you deserve? Welcome to a journey that promises not just transformation, but profound self-discovery. In a world filled with distractions and demands, finding time to focus on yourself can feel like an uphill battle. Yet, it's crucial to remember that the most powerful change begins from within.

I created *Bloom!* for every woman who has felt this struggle—for all of us seeking the resilience to navigate obstacles, reclaim confidence, and fully own our lives. As a coach, I've worked with thousands of women from diverse backgrounds, each with unique stories and yet so many common challenges. While I speak from my experience as a Black woman, *Bloom!* is for every woman who has ever felt sidelined, undervalued, or unable to fully step into her power.

As The Strategy Chick® I am known by friends and colleagues for always being ready with a plan. This became my personal brand after former Starbucks colleague Corey duBrowa told our agency team during a campaign launch, "If you need a strategy, CeCe is the one to call!" I believe a good strategy provides a sense of control and increases your ability to manage constant change.

Here, I've gathered stories of everyday people doing extraordinary things. Stories of remarkable women and men who have faced and overcome life's complexities, along with coaching tools and exercises that will help you on your journey of transformation. Together, these stories combined with my personal reflections on surviving alopecia, cancer and job loss, provide strategies to assist you with life's challenges, help you find strength in self-discovery, and encourage you to grow in ways that feel true to you. The end of each chapter includes "Golden Eggs," my sayings or words of wisdom, as well as lessons learned by each person. Feel free to share or use them to guide, affirm or support you in your growth. They are seeds that will help you find your strengths. It may not be easy, but self-empowerment is a muscle you can develop.

In *Bloom!*, I introduce a unique equation for self-empowerment based on the 3 F's–*Facing Yourself, Facing Change, and Facing Others*. In these initial chapters, you'll confront your inner truths, recognize your strengths, and create a vision for the future. The journey then leads to the 3 R's–*Relationships, Resiliency, and Reinvention*, focusing on your relationships with others, resilience in the face of setbacks, and the power of reimagining your path. Each step is designed to guide you in building a life that resonates with your true values and aspirations.

The tools, insights, and exercises here have supported many of my clients in strengthening their confidence, establishing presence, and overcoming obstacles to reclaim their personal power. I hope that, by working through these exercises, you'll discover your own powerful voice, redefine success on your terms, and embrace a life that reflects your worth and potential.

To everyone who has ever felt they needed to work twice as hard to be recognized, or struggled to silence their inner critic, know that you are not alone. This journey is about thriving on your own terms and building a future filled with purpose and power. Take this opportunity to invest in yourself, explore what you truly desire, and allow yourself to grow into the extraordinary woman you're meant to be.

So, let's get started. Visit my website www.thestrategy-chick.com and register to access all of the exercises and tools shared in this book. Set your intent, embrace the challenge, and let's redefine what it means to be powerful—not just in the eyes of others but in your own. Together, let's make this journey one of self-discovery, strength, and, ultimately, a celebration of everything you are capable of becoming.

Flowers bloom in their own season. Some lie dormant allowing other areas of the garden to prosper. Like the gardener, pull the weeds, keep nurturing all your seeds and every plant until it is your time to bloom.

Part I

THREE FACES OF SELF-EMPOWERMENT

GETTING OUT OF THE WEEDS

What does it mean to live a self-empowered life? Before defining your journey, you should be aware of the four common challenges women will experience at some point during their transformation. Most clients present with at least one or more during coaching engagements. These four challenges are comparable to weeds in your garden that weaken self-confidence and could prevent you from fully blossoming into your best self. They are: lacking vision and purpose, not seeing yourself as a leader, microaggressions that make you feel marginalized, and poor coping skills.

Addressing these upfront and clarifying the strategies necessary to provide a solid bed to plant seeds and kick-off your journey is where we are going to start.

Lacking Vision: Clarify Your "Why" and Define Your Purpose

One of my first clients, Robyn, an entertainment industry executive had recently returned from a successful international assignment that positioned her as the next Chief Marketing Officer. While her career was set on an upward trajectory, her return brought unexpected challenges. Soon after, she missed a key forecast—a slip that raised concerns among her managers and advocates about her readiness for executive roles. In a high-stakes environment with minimal tolerance for mistakes, Robyn felt the pressure mounting.

What was behind this shift? It wasn't her ability but her desire that had changed. Robyn was at a crossroads: single, turning 40, and increasingly longing to live closer to her family. The responsibilities of a high-profile role conflicted with her personal priorities, leaving her torn. She worried about the impact on her reputation and finances if she declined the promotion, yet she felt uncertain about committing fully.

Seeking clarity, Robyn turned to coaching, embarking on a journey of self-discovery to navigate these conflicting priorities. Through our sessions, she confronted her personal truths and made empowered decisions that aligned with her values.

How did we do this? By using a series of vision-setting, scenario planning and intentional change models, Robyn was able to shift her mindset and be more flexible to change.

1. Vision Setting: I asked Robyn to write a detailed story of what she would do if money were no object. Where would she live, how would she spend her time and with whom? What type of work would she prefer doing?

2. Scenario Planning: This involved creating 3-4 options of what "ifs" (probable outcomes) and creating a high-level plan for each one.

3. Intentional Change Theory: A self-directed learning process to help define your ideal self. Robyn started by sharing her personal vision with her inner circle. The feedback was useful in creating a sustainable plan where Robyn could feel supported in her vision for creating a new life.

Robyn was a highly valued executive. She leveraged her relationships to advocate for coaching and additional time to determine her next move. I partnered with Robyn to develop a clear strategy for moving forward. It helped her make the decision to ask the organization for a different job and full relocation benefits to be closer to her family. Although the assignment was a lateral switch into a different function, she could have the lifestyle she envisioned. By taking time to face herself, assess the risks and rewards, she could take decisive action and achieve what mattered most to her. Some of you reading this might ask, "Who has the luxury of taking the time to decide anything?" Instead, consider asking, "What will it cost me if I take a position I am not ready for?" Always advocate for what you need, it is a cardinal rule of being empowered.

This is Self-Empowerment. Proactively taking control of your life, making conscious decisions to direct and control your destiny. It is different than being self-confident. Confidence is an internal belief in your abilities. Empowerment is the result of using your abilities to make decisions which direct the course of your life and ability to achieve your goals.

I used this quick check list with Robyn to help guide her decisions. You can use it to jump start your journey towards self-empowerment.

Self-Empowerment Guide:

1. Make Choices: Self-empowerment starts with deciding to take control of your life and future. Be mindful of the decisions you make and where you want to go.
2. Positive Decisions: Self-empowered people usually choose things that match their values and goals. They focus on actions that help them grow, stay healthy, and succeed.

3. Take Action: It's not just about thinking—it is also about doing. To empower yourself, you need to work towards your goals. This might mean trying new things, taking risks, and staying strong when things get tough.

4. Believe in Yourself: Self-empowered individuals are confident in their abilities and trust their choices. They have the courage to go after what they want with determination.

5. Know Yourself: Understanding your strengths, weaknesses, values, and goals is important for self-empowerment. Self-empowered people know who they are, what they want, and what they can achieve.

6. Stay Motivated and Learn: Self-empowered individuals are driven to learn, develop, and grow. They believe in continuous improvement, both personally and professionally, and they keep learning throughout their lives.

7. Be Strong and Persevere: Shit happens. Tough times and challenges are part of life. Self-empowered individuals are resilient and keep going when faced with difficulties. They see setbacks as opportunities to learn and grow.

Overall, self-empowerment is about taking ownership of your life, embracing your potential, and actively working towards creating the future you desire. By cultivating self-awareness, confidence, and resilience, women can empower themselves to overcome obstacles, achieve their goals, and live a fulfilling and purposeful life.

Not Seeing Yourself as a Leader: Cultivate Your Inner Leader

The second challenge that diminishes your confidence and impact is not fully owning your role as a leader. Putting a stake in the ground and envisioning yourself as a leader is an effective way to integrate all segments of your life. Leadership is not just relegated to being in the workforce. All women are leaders in some capacity. Take a moment to complete the following Sphere of Influence exercise. You can also download it by visiting the resource section on my website. It will help you visualize how powerful you really are.

| SPHERE OF INFLUENCE EXERCISE |

Download this form and fill in the blank squares with the names of people who need or depend on you. You may include family members, work relationships, groups and organizations you support. Make your list as thorough as possible. Review it and use the space below the graphic to capture any emotions or thoughts that come to mind. This is a visual representation of your MIPs (Most Important People), your sphere of influence.

When I do this exercise with clients, they are always amazed at how significant and impactful their leadership is to others. Keep this list handy. Review it regularly to help prioritize your relationships and to remind yourself that you are powerful, you are very necessary, and you are a leader.

Seeing yourself as a leader can also help reframe how you think and stop the negative self-talk that comes from feeling excluded. It forms a basis for you to think about unconventional ways to use your leadership and skills. The ability to flex and reimagine yourself increases confidence and paves the way for believing your goals are achievable.

So now what? You have reviewed your list, you are feeling energized and powerful, you are skilled, educated, and ready. But it still feels hard. You feel like you are not making any progress, just repeating the same things, and going nowhere. I had one client compare it to feeling like a hamster on a wheel—running and running in a circle going nowhere. You are not alone and there is a very good reason for feeling this way. It is hard to live or work in a society where you feel undervalued.

The business case for diversity in corporations continues to evolve. It has moved from a focus on representation to one of inclusion. This dilutes the impact of DEI programs specifically tailored to supporting Black people. The impact of the Harvard case, where the Supreme Court eliminated race as an admission criterion, is already being felt in elite college enrollment showing a drop in the number of black freshmen. This decision effectively dismantled affirmative action and paved the way for many Fortune 500 companies to disband their DEI functions, eliminating positions traditionally held by women of color. As the pipeline shrinks, it underscores the need for you to have a vision and strategy to remain relevant, be open to new and different opportunities and fully embrace and use your strengths.

Microaggressions That Make You Feel Marginalized: Use Inquiry and Boundaries to Address Microaggressions

Let's face it, it is hard out here. I imagine, like me, you feel multiple forces vying for attention. As my career advanced, so did the demands on my time, and I often felt stretched too thin. Balancing parenting, caring for my mom, and striving to exceed expectations at work, I constantly felt the pressure to be perfect. This pressure felt intensified by a lingering sense that, as a black professional, I had less margin for error. It felt like I was being held to a higher standard and scrutinized more closely.

One experience stands out, I had crafted a speech and a comprehensive communications plan for a company-wide initiative, which received strong engagement and positive feedback. Yet, some leaders on the executive team seemed quick to pick apart my work—not for its substance but for minor stylistic choices that didn't seem relevant to the strategy's goals. I felt defensive and misunderstood, thinking about how my colleagues often faced different standards. I watched some receiving praise and promotions for efforts that didn't always yield results, while I was judged more intensely on seemingly trivial matters despite being a consistently strong performer.

This angered me and led me to question what I might be missing or whether I should just leave the company. Was there something I could do differently to shift these dynamics? This experience pushed me to reflect deeply, challenging me to dig deep and find resilience, refine my perspective, and ultimately set my boundaries and priorities more clearly. After all, it is no secret to anyone who is under-represented, that DEI means "**definitely earned it.**"

The answer came to me one evening while watching *The Hunger Games* movie. Mindset. The answer is mindset. In this dystopian trilogy, the ruling upper-class would start a battle between carefully selected leaders from the marginalized classes. Before the games began, they would say, "May the odds be ever in your favor." The truth is most people will not make it to the finish. It is a survival game with only a few opportunities for leaders who are not from the ruling class.

The heroine Katniss is from the marginalized district. She realizes her mindset must change to survive. I began cheering for her as she stepped into her full power. Her first important lesson was to help herself first. She had to know when to break the rules, who should stay on her team, and who had to be sacrificed. I recall needing to make similar decisions when on-boarding into a leadership position.

Think of a time in your life when you had to decide who to keep in your corner. You can use a similar strategy by creating your personal board of directors. People who you know are committed to supporting you and helping you advance.

Later, I realized the importance of shedding any victim mentality and embracing my past to increase my impact. This is similar to the movie's final symbolic message when Kat recognizes that her valuable survival skills came from being the underdog. When she emerges as the winner, Kat says, "Where you come from doesn't determine where you will go."

I believe adopting a similar mindset is necessary to thrive and fully embrace your power against headwinds. The odds are not in your favor. *Catalyst's 2023 U.S. Women of Color Report* shows that women of color will outnumber all women in 40 years. White males will continue dominating the workforce and hold most executive positions, and despite an increase in college graduates, more Black and Hispanic women will continue to be unemployed and underpaid.

The recent Harvard Decision, the landmark Supreme Court ruling to end race-based college affirmative action programs, paved the way for dismantling diversity, equity, and inclusion programs across the country. Women of color who led these initiatives are now out of work or in lower-level jobs. As the political climate shifts in the country and globally, you can expect to see significant changes impacting women's health and welfare.

It will be necessary to shift the focus from being victims of circumstance, to a growth mindset with new personal operating rules. Reframing questions is an excellent way to control "Automatic Negative Thoughts" (ANT). Here are a few questions to ask yourself when you need to shift to more positive thinking:

- "Am I overstating the problem or challenge?"
- "If this happened to my friend, how would I counsel them?"
- "What is another way to look at this?"
- "At the very least, I can do…"

I believe diverse women can win against the odds. By visualizing yourselves as leaders and making small changes to how you think about your challenges, you can set yourself up to get beyond the negativity.

Against the Odds: Managing Microaggressions

Even when you're in a job you love and your career is on the rise, microaggressions can still cast a shadow. Microaggressions—those subtle, slights or insults that reveal bias—can occur in both your personal and professional lives and have lasting impacts.

I vividly remember leading a pitch presentation for an ad campaign early in my career. I had written the creative brief, poured hours into developing the pitch, and rehearsed until every detail felt seamless. But when the clients arrived, the senior executive handed me his coat to hang up. Then, during my part of the presentation, he directed his questions to my white female colleague instead of me. These moments—being asked to perform a task unrelated to my role and then overlooked in my area of expertise—are examples of microaggressions.

At the time, I didn't know how to react. I feared that speaking up might label me as "difficult" or "aggressive." Without realizing it, I muted my own voice and allowed insecurities to hold me back from fully embracing my authority in the room. It wasn't until years later, as I trained to become a coach, that I understood how the intersection of my race, gender, and early experiences had influenced my leadership style and self-perception.

Microaggressions don't stop at work, they happen in all areas of life. Have you ever walked into a high-end store and felt "overlooked" by the sales associate or, worse, treated as though you might steal something? These interactions can be deeply painful, and we could all write chapters on the ways they impact us. But we do have strategies to manage these moments with dignity and confidence.

One effective way to respond is by using inquiry to calmly question the behavior. This approach can defuse the situation and prompt the other person to think about their actions. For instance, when that executive handed me his coat, I might have said, "Would you like me to find someone to help with that so I can focus on our meeting agenda?" A question like this both addresses the microaggression and refocuses attention on my role and expertise.

Microaggressions can also come in the form of unwelcome curiosity, often tied to personal attributes. Shortly after being diagnosed with alopecia, I decided to go natural and cut off my permed hair. When I returned to work with a short, cropped afro, a white colleague walked up behind me, started stroking my hair, and exclaimed, "Wow, it's so different from Friday! What did you do?" Though I was angry at her intrusion, I chose a calm response. "Have you ever seen a haircut?," I asked, then, after a pause, added, "Do you usually touch people's hair after it's been cut?" This shifted the conversation, leading her to apologize, and it gave me an opportunity to explain why her actions were offensive. I was able to turn a moment of frustration into a chance for learning and understanding.

Microaggressions are often subtle but powerful, impacting our confidence and sense of belonging. By using calm inquiry and thoughtful responses, we can manage these experiences, assert our dignity, and create opportunities for positive change.

Humor can be a powerful tool in disarming uncomfortable situations, and one memorable experience still makes me smile. In 1985, I was the only Black assistant account executive at Needham, Harper & Steers, one of Chicago's top ad agencies. One afternoon, the president, Dick Needham, and the executive director, Bob Savard, came into my office, shut the door, and sat across from me with somber expressions. They leaned in, speaking in hushed, urgent tones. "Cecilia, we have a real problem," one began. "We've been recruiting, but we just can't seem to find any Black men for account management roles."

Realizing they were obviously placing this burden on me, I leaned in too, mirroring their seriousness and adopting a conspiratorial whisper: "Well, if I knew where to find them, do you think I'd still be single?" The shock on their faces was priceless! After a stunned silence, we all burst into laughter, and it broke the tension in an unforgettable way. But one thing's certain—they never asked me a question like that again.

Most of us have felt the sting of microaggressions, whether subtle or blatant, and these experiences often linger. Leaning into these emotions can actually make us stronger, more empathetic leaders. And having an ally—a safe space to vent, strategize, and find perspective—can be invaluable, especially for women from marginalized backgrounds. This is one of the reasons coaching is so powerful; it creates that space for growth and resilience, turning our experiences into sources of strength.

Poor Coping Skills: Build Resilience with Intentional Coping Techniques

My journey toward embracing my power has been shaped by significant personal and professional challenges. From being the first Black girl to integrate my elementary school to overcoming alopecia and surviving cancer, each experience taught me how to cope with adversity and build resilience. Through these trials, I developed essential coping skills, such as problem-solving and emotional adaptability.

I viewed life through a lens of continuity, acknowledging that shit will happen, but getting the most out of the times when things are really great. It's the way I keep my glass half full. The good news? These skills can be learned, honed, and strengthened over time. Here, I'll share some powerful strategies that helped me and can support you in building resilience.

Two Foundational Coping Techniques:

- **Nurturing Strong Relationships**– People with higher Emotional Intelligence (EQ) are often those who have strong interpersonal connections, and relationships can be powerful buffers against stress. I learned from my parents to engage with people from all backgrounds, a skill that has been invaluable in managing life's challenges. Building a supportive network is a practical step toward strengthening your own coping skills.

- **Reflecting and Giving Back**– Reflecting on personal experiences and giving back are two practices that help redirect energy in meaningful ways. Not only do they foster a sense of purpose, but they also shift your mindset toward growth. The following stories illustrate how these practices have helped me cope with past traumas and align my values with my actions.

Giving Back through the Urban League

Growing up in Cleveland during the 1960s, I experienced several "firsts" that set the stage for my journey in resilience. It was 1966, the sounds of Motown could be heard on CKLW, an AM station, or WJMO, our local soul station.

Music was a refuge from the civil rights unrest blanketing the country. We lived in the Glenville section of Cleveland, with nice duplex houses on tree-lined streets where I played tag with my friends, rode my first bike, and learned to dance the boogaloo with my dad. Sleepovers with my best friends Cynthia and Kim, and mom's fresh skillet-made popcorn was a treat when we were allowed to stay up late and watch Gidget movies. This was my life, secure, happy, shielded from the violence and discrimination pulsing in the city.

However, my life changed abruptly when my father joined an Urban League program to integrate Cleveland's suburbs. I went from the safety of having classes and sleepovers with best friends who looked like me, to the isolation of being the "only." This was my early battleground for coping with exclusion. We became the first Black family in Euclid, Ohio, a move that came with media attention and unexpected challenges. It also opened new educational doors for me, preparing me to eventually be the first Black female student to graduate from Hawken, one of Cleveland's toniest private prep high schools. I was accustomed to being the first or only Black female individual in many situations, a good foundation for managing future corporate exclusion and inequities.

The Urban League's support and mission left a lasting impression on me. In high school, I designed my senior project around community service with the Urban League, tutoring underserved youth. Over the years, I stayed involved serving on boards and supporting youth reading programs. Giving back to the organization that helped lift my family out of the inner city remains a grounding force, helping me cope with the pain from racism by focusing on positive outcomes. This commitment aligns with my values and forms a foundation for my resilience, coping skills and desire to pay it forward.

A Reflection on Ruby Bridges and Me

My parents, Betty and Cecil, were driven to move north to Cleveland from the Jim Crow South in search of better opportunities. As young teen-aged parents, they faced significant odds to achieving the American dream. My dad eventually dropped out of college to care for his expanding family which included my older sister Cyndi. Their early educational experience was limited to attending a Rosenwald School. Developed by Julius Rosenwald, philanthropist and part owner of Sears Roebuck and Company, these one, two, or, three room schools were for all school aged Black children in Gibson County, Tennessee. They were designed to be "separate but equal" in the segregated south. However, they lacked the same resources and facilities reserved for white students in the same county. I recall dad telling me when he took chemistry in college, it was the first time he had been in a lab or used a microscope, petri dish or slides. Ironically, he went on to become a chemist, overcoming these initial roadblocks. I am certain I get much of my determination just from watching him.

The summer of '66, I visited my grandparents in Tennessee, it was 102 in the shade, and I was playing with my cousins in the cotton fields where my ancestors had sharecropped. Growing restless, I suggested going to a movie. As we walked to town, dry winds would blow particles of red clay dirt that would sting my legs. I imagined what life was like for my parents walking to school, watching as the buses filled with white children drove by.

I witnessed firsthand the barriers they faced, when I saw a "Whites Only" sign for the first time outside the movie theater. I stood in silence. I had never been forced to go through a separate door because I was Black. In retrospect, I see that my parents took me south that summer to prepare me for integrating Euclid public schools in the fall. I call this my "Ruby Bridges moment." Ruby was the first African American child to integrate an all-white Louisiana elementary school in 1960. She is also the subject of Norman Rockwell's famous painting, "The Problem We All Live With."

Although I did not have armed guards escorting me into school, at eight years of age, I modeled my parent's actions and knew I had the responsibility to pave the way for others. The experience left a lasting mark on me. I am sharing these details because there are many women, who, like me, are first in their families to achieve educational and corporate successes. Despite the generational divide, the impact of racism and sexism continues to thwart women's career aspirations. Storytelling serves as a good way to preserve history and remind us that it requires our collective efforts to keep momentum.

Reflecting on these early experiences reminds me of the resilience I needed then and continues to inspire me today. Facing those challenges helped shape my identity as a resilient Black woman, unafraid to enter any room and fill my seat with confidence. Reflection has become a powerful tool that strengthens my inner resolve and fuels my purpose. When I am facing difficult things and the shit seems endless, I close my eyes, and say, "I am not going down!" Open my eyes, breath deep and sing my walk-on song, Unstoppable.

Practical Reflection Tip: *To use reflection in shaping your own narrative, start by jotting down your experiences on*

Post-its. Organize them by themes or lessons learned and refer to them often to remind yourself of the strength you've gained along the way and incorporate them into your storytelling.

Commonly Asked Questions

As women, we encounter diverse challenges, yet we often share common questions and experiences. Whether it's about career decisions, leadership, or finding confidence, having a safe space to be vulnerable is essential. Here are three common questions that often arise:

Should I Stay or Should I Go?

When frustration with work or relationships arises, shifting from a "victim mindset" to personal accountability is essential. For example, Tanisha, a marketing director, initially felt her manager's feedback was biased. She had been described as difficult to work with due to her lack of organization, frequent tardiness to meetings, and struggles to complete projects. She felt targeted because of her race and was unable to take accountability for her situation and wanted to leave the company. It was clear Tanisha needed to do some inner work to be open to constructive criticism. I asked her what was in her power to control. Focusing on what she could control, helped reframe her perspective, take accountability, re-engage with her goals and reduce the impulse to leave.

Why Do I Feel Like I Am Not Enough?

Imposter syndrome is real. It can prevent you from leveraging your skills and value in personal and professional relationships. It is generally rooted in early childhood experiences which somehow left you feeling inferior. When I am presented with this question, I believe it is more effective to focus on actions to move forward than over analyzing the past. Take these steps when working through this challenge:

1. Identify the triggers. What situations or events make you feel insecure? Big life changes, meetings, being in large crowds, difficult or intimate conversation? Any or all of these are typical spaces that can trigger insecurity.

2. Ask yourself how true that emotion or thought is. For example, I would not speak up in some meetings because I thought other colleagues knew more than me and I would say something irrelevant. I asked myself, "How true is it that I have nothing of value to add to this meeting?" I then shifted by thoughts to what I could add versus what I did not know.

3. Give your imposter-emotion or insecurity a name. Personalization allows you to talk directly to the fear and begin to stop the behavior when it appears. I call my imposter Little CeCe. She appears when I am not being true to myself, speaking my truths and leading. She was developed at a time when I needed to feel safe. She protected me by muting my voice. When I feel her presence I tell her, "Girl, I got this. Don't need help today." She is persistent, after all she is me, but I can generally keep her in check.

Why Do I Feel Stuck?

Feeling stuck often stems from outdated beliefs and assumptions. Start by identifying whether these blocks are internal or external, then rewrite any old "rules" you've been following to create space for new possibilities. For example, if you believe you must work twice as hard for recognition, consider redefining success on your terms.

What old operating rules or assumptions are you using that need to be updated and how can you rewrite them? Here are some examples:

MINDSET GRID	
OLD THINKING	NEW MINDSET
I don't have enough experience.	My interpersonal skills are great, and I interview extremely well.
I need to stay in this marriage for the kids.	I deserve to be happy.
There is so much to do I have no time for myself.	It is ok to ask for help.
I have to do everything, so I don't have the luxury of time.	Be a little less perfect, delegate and share the responsibilities.

Identifying what is blocking you from acting, sets the stage for rethinking and shifting perspectives and behaviors. Adam Grant's book, *Think Again*, describes a process of detaching your past from your present, and your opinions from your identity. He suggests asking how much of your former self appears in the person you are today? How many of your past beliefs need updating?

Consider ways to apply this approach and rethink your possibilities. Use it to design a new vision or shed victim mentality to shift your energy.

 ## Golden Eggs

I promised earlier that I would lay a few "Golden Eggs" or my words of wisdom and wit at the end of each chapter. Here are four things to share as you kick off your season to *Bloom!*

1. Flowers bloom in their own time. Don't worry what's in someone else's garden, tend to your own.
2. Focus on your mindset. Weed through marginalization, microaggressions and self-doubt.
3. Think of a person from your past outside of your family who truly helped you. If you are able, send them a letter of appreciation. The simple act of acknowledging someone's impact on your life helps sustain your growth.
4. Pay it forward. Find someone to lift and inspire. Focusing on someone else is a great strategy for feeling good. It makes everyone feel that they are "enough."

1

FACING YOURSELF

I am gazing out of my office window on a semi-cloudy Saturday afternoon, experiencing writer's block, and wondering what to share that will be most helpful for your self-empowerment journey. The weather forecast initially said it would be a gloomy, overcast day. Suddenly the sky is moving, and patches of blue are pushing the gray clouds aside. Storm clouds blew away and my writer's block lifted as the bright sun emerged. Like the weather, life can be unpredictable. However, you can successfully lead an empowered life and thrive amidst the challenges. Begin by looking in the mirror. Are you coachable?

Can You Be Coached?

First, let us acknowledge that the most difficult part of the journey is getting started. Perhaps it is because it requires some form of self-reflection—not simply remembering an event or activity but understanding its impact, and what you learned from the experience. Reflections are a form of assessing ourselves, our beliefs and values, and behaviors. For some, self-discovery is an exciting process. However, for others the journey can surface memories triggering deeper insecurities. These are normal reactions, and you should allow yourself time to sit with your thoughts and give them the attention they deserve. Here are a few questions to help prepare you for taking the steps to a bolder, more confident you.

Assess Your Coachability:

Please follow these directions:

A. Using a scale of 1-10 with ten being the highest, answer each of the following questions honestly. Remember, there are no wrong or right answers.

B. Once you have completed scoring your answers, total your scores. You should end up with a number between 6 and 60.

C. To find your average score, divide your total by 6.

Questions:

1. Are you excited about the opportunity for personal and professional growth? Rate on a scale of 1-10.

2. On a scale of 1-10, how open are you to embracing new perspectives and making positive changes in your approach?

3. When it comes to taking responsibility for your actions and commitments, where do you rate yourself on the 1-10 scale?

4. Are you willing to step out of your comfort zone and explore areas where you could grow and improve? Rate your willingness on a scale of 1-10.

5. How would you rate your ability to be honest with yourself about your strengths and areas for improvement? Rate on a scale of 1-10.

6. When receiving feedback, how open are you to constructive criticism on a scale of 1-10?

Here's what your score may indicate:

- **A lower score (1-4)** suggests you may need additional time to feel psychologically safe with the process. You might be new to working with a coach or taking small steps toward leading yourself.

- **A mid-range score (5-7)** could indicate a need to develop a stronger vision and set clearer goals.

- **If your average score is 8 or higher**, congratulations! You are coachable and ready to move forward.

Remember, wherever you find yourself on this scale is perfectly okay. This is your transformation journey, and it takes place on your timetable.

After determining your coachability, it is time to explore the three distinct phases towards being empowered. They are *facing yourself, facing fear, and facing others*. We will begin with the hardest part, a deep and honest look at yourself. As you begin, start with the toughest thing first. By prioritizing the most difficult tasks, you will experience a greater sense of accomplishment when it is complete. If you are skeptical, try it on your never ending to do list. Put the challenging tasks first and focus 100% of your energy on them. Remove the minor ones. Go for quality not quantity. Celebrate each task as you complete it. I keep a cowbell in my office that I ring when I am proud of something I have done. You can establish your own reward system but make one. It serves as a reminder that you can do hard things!

FACING YOURSELF

Masks, Mirrors, and Filters:
Who You See is Not Always Who You Get

In 1970, comedian Flip Wilson coined the iconic phrase, "Whatcha' see is whatcha' get!", a testament to raw authenticity. However, in today's digital age dominated by platforms like LinkedIn, Instagram, and Facebook, appearances can be deceiving. Women of color often find themselves navigating a delicate balance between self-expression and societal expectations, leading to a curated version of themselves in professional settings.

When coaching executive women, I frequently encounter a glaring disparity between perception and reality. Initial feedback from managers often paints a limited and distorted picture, overlooking the nuanced performance details crucial for effective coaching and personal growth. Despite outward appearances of assimilation and conformity, these women are often grappling with the burden of unexpressed emotions and a constant need to conceal their true identities.

This facade not only hinders their personal well-being but also undermines their leadership potential. Through establishing a foundation of trust and safety in our coaching sessions, I create a space for these women to shed their masks and reveal their authentic selves.

Removing the Masks: A Guided Exercise

Facing yourself requires inner and outer work. Experience breakthrough moments using guided visualization exercises to simulate removing layers and burdens. I have created one for you to use at home. I recommend doing it physically, but you have the option of using the simulated format. Follow these two steps to get started. First, using your phone, record the following paragraph. Next, playback the recording and follow the instructions step-by-step:

"Look into the mirror. Imagine you are going to remove your filters. If you are wearing make-up, take it off. Remove your jewelry, clothing, hair ornaments, and anything else until you are naked. Just you and the mirror. How does this feel? Now let's go a bit further. Put all labels aside. Your job title, strip it off. Are you mom, wife, husband, partner, sister, patient—any label that is used to describe you, simply lift, and gently drop them to the floor like rose petals. Who do you see in the mirror? She is the woman you want to talk to. She is the woman often standing between you and your greatness."

Consider the lenses through which you view yourself. What filters shape your self-perception and guide your judgments? Reflect on how much of your day is spent hiding behind these filters versus embracing your true, unfiltered self. Standing in front of the mirror, what aspects of yourself do you cherish the most? Initiate a practice of self-affirmation by vocalizing your appreciation for these qualities. Proudly celebrate yourself.

I encourage you to engage in this reflective exercise and document your insights and emotions. This practice serves as a grounding tool, aiding in maintaining focus as you delve deeper into exploring your intrinsic character traits and core values. By fostering a habit of positive self-affirmation and introspection, you can navigate the journey of self-discovery with clarity and authenticity, paving the way for personal growth and empowerment.

The power of positive self-talk should not be underestimated. Have you ever noticed how a negative thought can intrude on your productivity or change your mood? How might this impact your leadership? Truly empowered people know when to use positive self-talk to shift their energy and mindset.

Another warm-up exercise you can use is sharing a story describing the most courageous thing you have ever done. Provide context such as timing, why you engaged in this activity and how it made you feel. This process helps to see yourself in a different light.

1. Many people do not see themselves or what they do as courageous.
2. Women will downplay the significance of their courageous acts for fear of appearing boastful.
3. Most people think courage must be demonstrated on a large-scale, forgetting that the smallest gestures in daily living can take the most courage.

Can you use your courageous story as a foundation to bolster more confidence? Whenever you experience times of self-doubt reflect on moments when you were on fire, unstoppable. It does wonders to bring perspective on how badass you truly are!

Assessments: Facing Yourself

My corporate career was not a straight path. I progressed through sheer grit, some intelligence, and strong interpersonal skills. I first learned the power of formal assessments when I became a leadership coach. I observed that high potential talent was selected and groomed for future opportunities using leadership assessments, advocacy and stretch assignments. I also noted there were few women of color in this pipeline. You should make yourself aware of the different assessments your companies use and ask to include them as part of your growth plan. Chances are, if you are not being assessed, you are not being tracked for promotion.

Self-Assessments— You should always begin with knowing yourself. There are many self-help tools you can use to assist you.

1. Values— Create a list of your top 5 values. Here are some examples: authenticity, curiosity, resiliency, compassion, empathy, loyalty, trust, security etc.

2. Skills inventory— What are your superpowers? List them and compare it to what others say about you.

3. Stakeholder Perceptions— Using your sphere of influence list from Chapter 1, ask people on your list to describe you. Group these adjectives and compare them to your self-perception. If there is a wide difference, go back to the person and ask for more clarity on how they view you. This feedback can be helpful in identifying blind spots in your personal brand and image.

Personality Assessments— There are many different types of personality tests. Some are free and available online. Myers Briggs, DISC, The Big Five, and True Colors are also used by companies to evaluate cultural fit.

Leadership Assessments– This group of assessments are generally reserved for high potential talent and top performers to evaluate their leadership capabilities. Combined with 360 feedback, they give insights into your strengths, opportunity areas and blind spots to enhance your leadership. They are used by coaches and trained providers to interpret and deliver results. Frequently part of a full development program, they are expensive and a strong indicator the company is willing to invest in you. Hogan Assessments, Birkman, Korn Ferry, and other consultancies have customized leadership evaluations. Familiarize yourself with the ones your company uses and ask to be evaluated. If you are self-employed or want to understand more about your leadership style, consider hiring a certified executive coach.

The Psychology of Coaching

Looking back, I have always been fascinated with human behavior. I wanted to know where personality came from; were you born with it or did it develop over time. What makes someone introverted while other people are more outgoing? How could my colleagues process financial data and ask questions faster than me? Honestly, I was asking why can they do something that I cannot? How can I do more or improve?

Many studies have been conducted on nature versus nurture behavior theories. But I wanted to learn the processes achievers use to overcome obstacles and translate them into strategies to thrive. Eventually this curiosity would lead me to create an easily repeatable framework and help clients step into their power.

My first exposure to psychology and therapy came at an early age. Dad was a janitor at University Hospitals of

Cleveland shortly after moving up north and worked in Hanna Pavilion, the psychiatric hospital. As a precursor to "Take Your Daughter to Work Day," he occasionally would take me to meet all the doctors and nurses on his floor.

Mom would dress me in my Sunday patent leather Mary Jane shoes and white ankle socks with lacy ruffles. Adorned with a colorful outfit and matching hair ribbons my mom would press and weave into my four pigtails. He was so proud of me, always smiling and telling everyone how smart I was. Sometimes when I am really struggling to work through something, I reflect on a positive event or memory to help shift my energy. This memory always works for me!

Ironically, this led to my major in psychology and my first summer intern position. I wanted to be a clinical therapist. I thought it was a perfect blend of altruism and my gift of gab. During college, I interned in the hospital working with severely depressed patients and tutoring autistic children. Much of the teaching process involved sensory and inter-active scaffolding, customized to help students learn at their level. Many of the techniques to help patients move forward are applicable in everyday life.

The Process

These combined experiences influence the approach I use to help people realize their potential to do remarkable things. I call it STRAT:

Shave the layers – Assess who you are.

Talk – Create the "T" zone – a safe place to bond, share and face your roadblocks.

Reimagine – Vision, dreaming and mindset shifting.

Act – Planning and goal setting!

Thrive – Tracking your progress against your goals.

Think of a behavior or habit you would like to change. What happens when you share your goals or ideas about this change with others? Research shows that you are more likely to be successful and sustain the shift when you publicly share your commitment to the goal. The act of vocalizing your vision and goals biologically rewires the process in your brain. Overtime, this becomes a sustainable habit. This is the neuroscience behind brain-based coaching. Or simply stated, "If you think it, you can do it!"

If you are new to coaching, you might wonder about the difference between coaching and therapy. Coaching focuses on actions to overcome present challenges for future success, while therapy addresses past trauma and emotional issues through clinical methods. Sometimes, individuals benefit from both coaching and therapy. I have collaborated with therapists to assist clients, especially those facing challenges like time management or emotional regulation. It's important to utilize all available resources to support your personal growth.

If you are still nervous about coaching and its benefits, you may find inspiration in these next stories of women owning their power by facing themselves.

Kathy Fernando, Ph.D., Senior Vice President and Global Head of Pfizer Ignite

Brown, Bisexual, and Badass!

Women of color often find it challenging to manage their image and brand in environments where they are obviously different.

Meet Kathy Fernando, a trailblazing Senior Vice President at Pfizer, whose leadership evolved over the span of six trans-formative years and two promotions during our coaching journey. Kathy is a South Asian woman of color with a brilliant scientific mind. No stranger to hardships, Kathy's formative years were far from conventional as she traversed the bus-tling streets of the Bronx to the tranquil landscapes of Sri Lanka before seeking refuge in India amidst the turbulence of civil unrest. Rooted in the teachings of her traditional Indian upbringing that prioritized education, hard work, and humility, Kathy's intellect and motivation endeared her to her mother, who had challenged societal norms and earned a medical degree at the age of 45 after having three children.

As Kathy completed her education, she felt societal pressure to marry and conform to gender norms in Indian culture. This pressure heightened her awareness of gen-der disparities making her personal and professional lives difficult to navigate.

During our first intake session, Kathy shared why she chose me as her coach, "From the beginning you committed to helping me learn how to thrive as my authentic self." I also asked Kathy to tell me the most courageous thing she had ever done. Without hesitation, she replied, "Coming out to my dad as a bisexual woman in 2016." This was a pivotal moment in our coaching relationship. I had deep empathy for her and appreciation for the pain she had been living with. "Kathy, what was different for you in 2016 that made it the right time to come out to your dad?"

"By then I was married with two boys. I met my husband while completing my Ph.D. at the University of Pennsylvania. We shared similar passions in life and a desire to forge a strong, meaningful and supportive relationship. We balance each other and he is a calming force for me. Marrying him was the best decision I ever made. My sexual orientation was a non-issue for him. He understood my perfectionist qualities and he is the biggest champion of my career." At this point, her entire posture and facial expressions relaxed. I knew this part of her story was key to unlocking her authentic leadership.

"The 2020 election made me think differently about discrimination. In India, class and gender marginalization were the dominant issues. But the election made me realize how little I knew about American civil rights. My concerns grew and I felt more nervous about raising two brown young men and being bisexual. We made a family trip to the African American Museum in Washington D.C. to learn more about the impact of marginalization on black people. The experience changed the way I thought about being different. I felt proud of myself, and my heritage and I wanted to be more vocal about who I am as a person." This defining moment in Kathy's life gave her the courage to come out to her dad.

I watched Kathy continue shedding the filters she wore as she let her guard down. I could see her genuine warmth and empathy emerging. This would become part of her leadership vision, and together we crafted a holistic coaching plan to strengthen her confidence and build better personal relationships at work.

Kathy had received feedback that her leadership could be more inspirational. The rigid approach and scientific curiosity which made her successful in management consulting did not translate well in her new corporate position. She was advised to improve her interpersonal skills, be more approachable and, yes, vulnerable. Her perfectionist tendencies made her team feel micromanaged. Talking with her colleagues revealed they did not know her well and thought she lacked self-awareness of how her style was perceived.

Working with Kathy was exciting. She was coachable and committed to the process. After conducting a lengthy history intake session, we focused on her vision of leadership and what was holding her back. I led Kathy through a series of assessments and exercises to help her unmask and learn what was keeping her from fully embracing her power. Like many women of color, Kathy believed focusing on work alone would be enough to advance. It was also a coping mechanism she used to keep from oversharing and protecting her vulnerability at work.

We finally cracked through this veneer preparing for Kathy's new leader assimilation workshop with her team. This was an excellent opportunity for her to deepen connections with her team. During the workshop, the team could ask questions to learn more about her values, vision and influences on her leadership.

I shared the questions with Kathy and helped her prepare her responses, encouraging her to be open and authentic. By creating smaller steps in the process, or chunking, it was easier for Kathy to feel comfortable and be naturally engaged. She used this time to reveal more about herself, including being bisexual, which over time led to being more vocal about being bisexual at work and supporting other leaders who had similar challenges. It is exciting to see Kathy fully embracing who she is and step into her power. Pfizer provided a conducive atmosphere for Kathy to grow and thrive as her authentic self.

Coaching supported Kathy in her journey by matching her need for details, strategy and planning, with a structured process that provided her with a sense of control. She faced herself through assessments and grew more comfortable with being her authentic self with her colleagues, fully stepping into and owning her power and she is now in full *Bloom!*

It is challenging for women of color to be authentic in professional settings. They often feel judged or that their voice won't matter. I asked Kathy to share reflections on authenticity and self-empowerment that you might find helpful.

"Don't place artificial constraints on what you can do." Changing your mindset is the first step towards being self-empowered.

"Maintain a relentless pursuit of self-improvement." This is one of the attributes my husband admires about me when he summarizes my growth.

"There is great joy and power in sharing and being your authentic self. It makes the work more enjoyable, and it amplifies your impact."

You may be in a similar situation trying to determine how to lead authentically at work or at home. Always start by facing yourself and assessing what is holding you back. Create a vision, shift your mindset, find your sweet spot, and go for it! Remember, you've had the power all along.

Hair Today, Gone Tomorrow: How I Faced Alopecia

This last story of self-acceptance is my personal battle with alopecia. I know there are many women dealing with hair loss and its impact on their psyche. I want you to know that you can find a new and better you by embracing these changes. Facing alopecia in my mid-forties, my hair began thinning after my youngest daughter Cammy's birth. The burning sensation of my follicles dying left me feeling insecure with a shining scalp that grew more prominent over time. This change deeply affected my self-esteem, because hair has always been viewed as a woman's crowning glory, sense of attractiveness, and femininity.

I sought emotional support through counseling and tried various remedies to reverse the hair loss, but to no avail. Wigs became a regular accessory, even as I experimented with unique styles to maintain a natural look. The deeper emotional issue I needed to address was facing my image in the mirror, and accepting the natural beauty in my features. When I saw my naked reflection, the trauma from being taunted for my wide nose, skin color and nappy hair in elementary school returned. It took me eight years to gather the courage to accept myself, embrace the change, and cut my hair into a close-cropped style. When my friend and stylist Darryk Floyd completed the big chop, I could feel the weight of the old insecurities fall away like the dead hair. I was free! Re-defining my style with new accessories and makeup, I proudly revealed my transformation to my daughters.

However, reactions were mixed, ranging from curiosity to misunderstanding. A stranger at the store mistook my hair transformation for a health issue, while Cammy flatly commented, "Mom, you look like a boy."

"No, I don't. I look like a woman with short hair," I firmly responded. I showed the girls how I had more time for them and embraced new hobbies because I spent less time on my hair. I went on to express that a woman's beauty, femininity, and intelligence are not defined by her hair, and I shared India Arie's empowering song "I Am Not My Hair" to teach them the same valuable lesson I demonstrated through my actions.

Cammy's statement triggered a profound realization within me. I understood the importance of shifting my mindset alongside transforming my hairstyle. This moment of clarity liberated me from insecurities related to my baldness, empowering me to confidently command attention in any room with my executive presence. Redirecting the time and money once dedicated to my hair, I focused on fitness by joining a club and rediscovering the joy of swimming. Embracing this transformative choice, I now find fulfillment in supporting other women navigating similar challenges. The unexpected surprise is that Cammy, a mirror image of me, now proudly sports a hairstyle like mine.

This is the neuroscience of coaching at its best. A self-directed effort to change my thoughts and behavior for my happiness. You can apply these steps outlined in my Golden Eggs to your goals and create your path to power and confidence.

 Golden Eggs

1. Face and embrace all of you. The body and mind are one. When you strengthen one part, everything benefits.
2. Just be yourself. You can't be somebody else.
3. Use STRAT: Repeat the following steps until you are in full bloom!

   Shave the layers– Assess who you are.

   Talk– Create the "T" zone– a safe place to bond, share and face your roadblocks.

   Reimagine– Vision, dreaming and mindset shifting.

   Act– Planning and goal setting!

   Thrive– Tracking your progress against your goals.
4. Get a coach!

2

FACING CHANGE

Change is a broadly studied topic discussed in science, music, and religion, all seeking to explain its considerable influence on our lives. The word change can evoke a range of emotions. The two most common emotions associated with change are fear and anxiety, even if the change is positive. I will first explore the physical effects of fear and anxiety, and quick ways to momentarily reduce stress. Then I will examine why change yields anxiety and share stories and strategies you can use to cope with change.

I enjoy listening to all kinds of music, whether it is R&B, jazz, rock, or country. Regardless of the genre, change is a common theme in many songs. You might hear about waiting for change like in John Mayer's song, "Waiting on the World to Change" or feel the soul stirring emotion in Sam Cooke's "A Change is Gonna' Come." For me, it was Nina Simone's spine-tingling rendition of "Everything Must Change" that really hit home. As a cancer survivor, the lyrics, "the young become the old," has greater significance. It is the realization that simply living makes change a constant.

There are many reasons for feeling anxious about personal or professional transitions. When you choose to make a change, like changing jobs, moving, starting a family, or getting married, you are in the driver's seat. But when changes are forced upon you by things out of your control, like the pandemic, being laid off, or a sudden health challenge, you can feel powerless.

Is It Fear or Anxiety: The Physiology of Stress

Understanding the difference between fear and anxiety can help you manage your reactions to situations which make you feel powerless. Fear is a naturally occurring emotion beginning within the brain. Our brains are hardwired to signal the body when it is in danger. When the brain registers fear, it quickly processes to determine what action we need to take to remain safe. These reactions are categorized into four responses; fight, flight, freeze, or fawn.

Fear Responses

The fight response can be physical or verbal. In physical altercations when there is real threat of bodily harm, the brain quickly decides if you can win. In verbal battles, you might experience anger and want to respond, but it is usually best not to react in these situations. For example, if a driver cut you off on a crowded expressway, almost causing you to crash, what would you do if he proceeds to get out of his car and curse you out with a lot of road rage? How would your body react if you sensed danger? Would you fight or would you flee?

The flight response sizes a situation and determines it is best to remove yourself from danger. It is a natural reaction when your brain detects a situation you cannot win. This might be demonstrated by actually getting up and leaving a room or disengaging from the conversation or changing the subject.

Freezing is the third fear response. In this case, the brain is directing the body to be very still. This could take the form of slow breathing, inability to speak or paralysis until the danger has passed.

The final fear response is fawning, also known as the people-pleasing response. This reaction is often observed in trauma and abuse victims. For example, abused women frequently apologize or over compliment their abuser to avoid conflict.

Anxiety

Remember, fear responses are not in your control. It is your brain's natural reaction to protect you from an external threat or danger. Now imagine your brain is constantly reacting in fear response mode when there is not a real threat or danger. This is anxiety.

Even though these terms are used interchangeably, understanding this difference can help you handle change more effectively. Fear is an automatic response to an external threat or danger, while anxiety is more internal and more vague. It's that uneasy feeling you get when you are worried about what might happen, whether it's something real or just in your head. According to the American Psychological Association (APA), anxiety involves feelings of tension, worried thoughts, and physical changes like increased blood pressure.

Anxiety produces stress which elevates levels of adrenaline and cortisol, the stress hormone. Consider the impact this stress has on your body. You've all been there. Heart racing, pulsating so hard you hear the internal bass drum in your ears. Your palms might be drenched in perspiration. Your face becomes flushed with heat and your mind is firing off with anticipation of what will happen next. Your tongue can feel so thick no words will form, but saliva is increasing, and you can almost taste the anxiety. And from that moment on, you begin to imagine every combination of outcomes, and become immobilized, unable to make progress and move forward. This is also the point where you might begin a narrative that you aren't good enough, a form of imposter syndrome.

Stress Diary

Keeping a stress diary is a good tool for managing your stress and reactions. You can design it to capture the most important things you want to track. You might start with:

1. Date and time
2. Describe the event
3. Identify your triggers
4. Your reactions (both physical and verbal)
5. A metric– rate your stress level on a scale, measure your heart rate or blood pressure

Review your stress diary over time and develop alternative solutions to your reactions. Reframe the narrative that you tell yourself about your stress to begin minimizing its impact and give you a greater sense of control.

Once your brain determines that you're not in immediate physical danger, fear transitions into anxiety. Signs of stress and anxiety can be seen both inside and outside your body. Internal symptoms include high blood pressure and heart rate, which can increase the risk of cardiac diseases or cancer. External symptoms of stress are the things you do when facing tough situations. For example, habits like nail-biting or fidgeting can be signs of stress. However, there are other behaviors that can affect how others see you and your effectiveness as a leader. These include having trouble focusing, being indecisive, acting stubborn, or being easily irritated with others.

In 360 survey interviews I use for client assessments, friends and colleagues often mention these behaviors when describing how leaders react to stress. Sometimes, you might not realize how stress is affecting your daily life. Not everyone shows the same signs of stress, so getting advice or feedback can help you identify these blind spots, making you feel more in control of your situation.

A recent study from the University of Pennsylvania found that about 90% of the things people worry about never actually happen. Just think about all the time and energy you've spent fretting over things that are unlikely to occur! Imagine how much more productive and empowered you could feel if you redirected that energy towards things, you could influence and control.

The next time you are anxious about a pending change in your life, use this to reframe your thoughts. It is easier to say, "I am anxious about changing versus, I am afraid to change." This slight but important mindset shift will give you a greater sense of accountability and control over your choices.

High anxiety and stress management is a concern and should be a priority for women of color, who have a higher probability of developing health-related conditions.

Here are three short-term strategies you can use to restore some balance and relief when your anxiety feels overwhelming.

Begin with identifying your triggers. What situations, words or people cause you to feel anxious. Knowing this ahead of time helps you take charge. You can delay conversations until you feel better or set boundaries with people who stress you out quickly.

Use the 333 rules. This is a simple counting technique commonly used for dealing with anxiety. It aims to help you calm down and regain control when feeling over-whelmed. To practice the 333 rules, you identify 3 things you see in your surroundings, recognize 3 sounds you hear, and touch or move 3 things, like objects or parts of your body.

Practice mindfulness. This is a form of stress reducing meditation which uses breathing techniques and guided imagery to calm and relax the mind and body. There are many easily accessible ways to practice mindfulness. Just creating a quiet safe place to do a self-check-in can help you think clearly and reduce anxiety.

Although these methods will not eliminate anxiety com-pletely, they can serve as a practical tool to cope with it in the moment.

"Turn and Face the Strange…" Why Change Evokes Anxiety

David Bowie's classic song "Changes" suggests that per-sonal growth is best achieved by embracing and adapting to unexpected challenges in life. Uncertainty is a common trigger for anxiety. Change inherently involves uncertainty, which explains why even positive changes can evoke anxiety.

Fear of Change or Imposter Syndrome?– Andrew's Dilemma

"Congratulations Andrew, you will be our next regional executive vice president!" During the past year, Andrew had imagined how exciting it would feel to hear these words. He had worked hard to earn this promotion. "I was thrilled, but I immediately began feeling anxious when I thought about all the changes and what this position would require."

"Andrew, congratulations! This is a moment to celebrate you. But I sense your apprehension. What is concerning you the most?"

"The position requires relocating to New York. I worry about the impact on my family. We can't afford the east coast. We have been in the south our entire married life, raising three kids and staying close to family. My wife has a fantastic job, and our village is strong. We cannot move east and expect to maintain our lifestyle. I know it will position me well in my career and I will have a chance to work in the fashion district, but I am afraid it will not be so great for everyone else."

Just like that, Andrew had jumped down the proverbial rabbit hole. Imagining every possible catastrophic outcome and minimizing the possibilities. Each sentence brought a heightened level of anxiety until I intervened to calm him down. The final concern he shared seemed to be the real source of his anxiety. "I will present to the board of directors, all financials, store plans and strategies. These are some of retail's most notable people. I am afraid I won't fit." This is a form of imposter syndrome.

Andrew began his career as an assistant buyer and rose through the ranks to lead one of the highest grossing departments in the company. He never imagined that he would one day manage a store he once walked through with his mom shopping for Christmas toys as a boy. Andrew came from humble beginnings which made him feel as though he was not "enough."

Andrew had two challenges, fear of change and imposter syndrome. It is not unusual to face multiple challenges and high levels of anxiety simultaneously. To prevent becoming overwhelmed, try isolating the issues and connecting to your higher purpose and vision. You can redirect your anxiety by focusing on a time or problem you successfully managed and had a positive outcome.

When Andrew reflected on a time he was feeling his best, most powerful self, he described the steps he took to manage the flagship store in his district and why it worked. Talking about this successful time in his life helped restore his calm and control.

What things resonated with you reading Andrew's story? What do you think he should focus on? Thinking of solutions to other people's challenges can help you be more creative in solving your problems when you feel you've reached an impasse.

Focus, Focus, Focus

Being a high achiever, Andrew harbored a fierce competitive drive and was afraid of failing, an emotion shared by many accomplished individuals who grapple with anxiety. This anxiety often manifests in excessive work, self-doubt, and impostor syndrome, which can lead to analysis paralysis.

Andrew, focused on understanding what triggers increased his anxiety.

Andrew followed this series of steps to restore his sense of control and move forward. You can use these or any process that helps during anxious periods.

1. Acknowledge the Anxiety: Assess your level of anxiety and consider seeking professional help, prioritizing your well-being above everything. I helped Andrew develop a list of triggers for his anxiety and name a correlating positive outcome for each negative thought. It made it easier to articulate his concerns with his wife and support system.

2. Prioritize: Using the wheel of life, categorize and rank your concerns across various areas such as career, finances, and relationships. The second chart is completed with shaded sections indicating the most important categories for this individual. You can fill in the sections and customize it to fit your priorities. Share and discuss these priorities with a trusted individual such as a partner or family member. Andrew eventually used this with his wife to align on their goals.

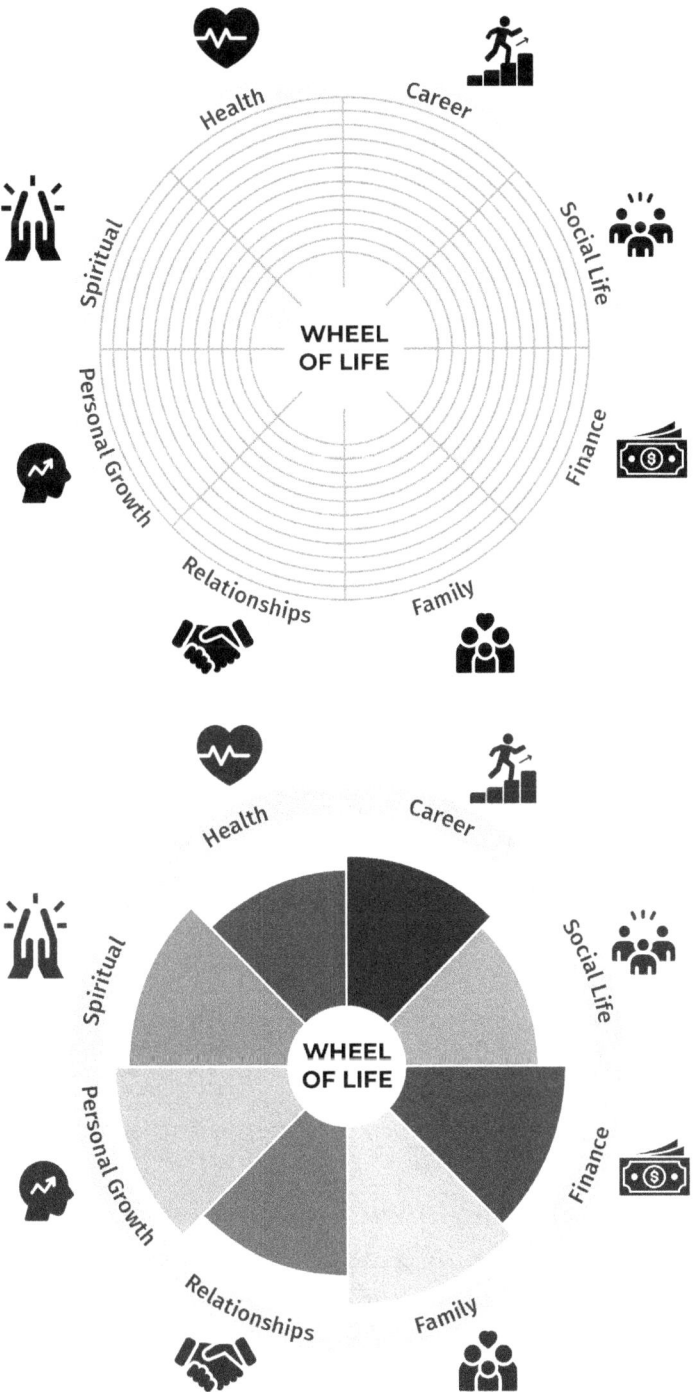

3. Plan for the Worst. Identify your anxieties and outline the worst-case scenarios, their likelihood, and strategies to minimize their impact. Consider seeking legal or professional advice if needed, like Andrew did when planning for his potential promotion and relocation.

4. Envision and create. Take the time during transformation to create a vision board or update an existing one, setting goals and aspirations visually. Engage in the process to gain clarity and motivation as Andrew did with his family.

5. Just say yes! Sometimes the best way to overcome anxiety is to take a leap of faith and say yes to new opportunities or challenges.

Andrew decided to accept the promotion but opted not to immediately relocate his family. Instead, he and his wife chose to stay until the end of the school year to maintain stability for their sons while he commuted. This arrangement provided the family with a sense of control and allowed them to navigate the transition more comfortably.

Just Say Yes!

Claim your power by making conscious decisions to shape your own path. Stepping out of your comfort zone and pushing past feelings of anxiety can ignite a greater sense of confidence.

"But what if I fail?" Anxiety about failing can hold you back. When you feel anxious, look for patterns that can include procrastination, concerns about others' opinions, or unexplained physical symptoms. If you see these are preventing you from performing at your peak, reprioritize and communicate with people closest to you and seek additional help if necessary.

Reflecting on your inner self, is a good place to start understanding the origins of this fear. Journaling is a good method to reflect and examine past experiences, both good and challenging, which shaped your confidence and self-esteem. These reflections offer valuable insights and effective strategies to move you forward.

Trish

Trish's story sheds light on a familiar struggle. A picturesque life in a dual career marriage with two kids, Trish faced uncertainty when her 15-year marriage dissolved, crushing her confidence, and leaving her with a deep sense of shame. The weight of disappointing her parents, who had modeled a successful union, added to her burden.

Trish withdrew from her support network, as she navigated the complexities of her new reality. Her reluctance to engage socially, fueled by fear of judgment and rejection, led her to decline invitations and isolate herself from opportunities for connection and growth. This was especially concerning because her position at a prominent law firm required high levels of engagement, face-time, and interpersonal skills.

Recognizing the signs of depression, Irish's loyal friends rallied together to provide the support and intervention she desperately needed. They suggested adding life coaching to her current work with her therapist.

Like many women who've been divorced, Trish tied her worth to old ideas and ways of living and had difficulty reimagining her life. She needed time to rethink her life and rediscover her why. Her friends cheered her on to take small steps—from working out together to chilling with Netflix and small dinners together—until she felt ready to socialize on a larger scale again. Although not dating yet, Trish was making strides by trying new things, shedding shame, and embracing social outings.

Trish later revealed that her close-knit group of friends played a vital role in her journey to overcome anxiety and change. They provided a supportive environment for her to envision a brighter future without judgement. With their encouragement, she re-entered the cycle of corporate events and other social activities without feeling insecure because she was divorced.

Trish's story is one that resonates with several women. While everyone's story is different, the common thread is facing change, anxiety, and learning how to create a new version of yourself.

I remember feeling anxious following my divorce. My priorities were the kids and work. I temporarily lost the ability to dream about my future. I could not imagine socializing or dating. Gradually, by assessing my values, strengths and needs, I used a vision board to create a new blueprint for my life.

Taking the first step by saying yes, is the hardest part of moving forward. How would you approach a major change in your personal life? You can use one of the blank journal pages in the resource section of my website to write your steps and reference it as needed. Sometimes it is easier to plan for change before it happens.

The Affirmation Jar

Create a jar of positive things people have said about you. Also include things you like about yourself. When you are facing major change and things feel out of your control, reach in the jar and read the positive quotes or words. Remember you are powerful, and this is just a moment in time.

Who Will I Be Today?

When faced with anxiety and uncertainty, I often recall a memory of my daughter Chandler at age 10–fearless, funny, and full of life. I remember the day she wore a bright red wig from her Scooby-Doo Daphne Halloween costume to school. Unfazed by others' opinions, she wholeheartedly embraced her playful choice and new identity. Reflecting on her carefree spirit and these wise words from her teacher,

"She is simply trying on new selves." These words still resonate with me after all these years and remind me to shift my perspective with fresh eyes.

Imagine living life as a child, unrestricted and free to explore any version of yourself. How many different personas would you try on? What dreams would you pursue? Embracing the excitement of reinvention is a strategy which allows me to let go of future worries and welcome change as a constant in my life. By channeling this childlike curiosity, I empower myself to conquer fears and shape my own path, celebrating the essence of self-empowerment.

I started this chapter with a musical touch, exploring the theme of change. As we near its end, let's tune into another little melody that beautifully reflects on the future with a light-hearted spirit. "Que Sera, Sera," sung by Doris Day, tells us to let things be and don't take life too seriously. Just ride it out and see what happens.

 **Golden Eggs**

1. Flowers bloom in their own time. There is a flower for every season. Your bloom does not have to match anyone else's.
2. The magic of growing up is that if we are lucky, it never stops. Embrace change with the curiosity of a child.
3. Friends are the family we chose. Choose wisely. Relationships are foundational to empowered people.
4. Just say yes!

3
FACING OTHERS

What does facing others mean? Simply put, it is the ability to communicate, connect with people, and build strong interpersonal relationships and support networks which increase your social capital and personal power.

Interpersonal Skills

Many people seek support to develop their interpersonal skills. These include verbal and non-verbal communications, listening skills, empathy, and attitude. The focus areas may differ between gender, generation, and race. For example, the Gen X and Millennial clients seek coaching support to strengthen their verbal communications. They are typically more advanced in their use of technology, virtual communications, and social media. Their focus areas include regulating emotions, reading verbal cues and using direct communication. This is also a sensitive area for women of color.

Gaining clear actionable feedback on how others perceive and experience you is essential to your success. When companies hire me for a new engagement, I can tell from the coaching brief the potential client is a woman of color. As a Black female coach, I can detect when managers are uncomfortable having difficult feedback conversations with women of color. Instead, they will expect coaching to deliver the feedback. When I encounter these situations, I strategically use inquiry and transparency to challenge the manager and set my client up for success. I will ask managers if they have directly communicated their observations to my client. If the answer is no, I probe more to learn why. Eventually, managers must hold themselves accountable for providing actionable feedback.

I have also observed microaggressions and bias in performance reviews. These moments provide an opportunity to leverage my corporate experience to create teaching opportunities to educate both clients and their managers. This comparison chart compiles a few common themes and descriptions I have observed managers use for women of color versus white women:

Frequently Used Quotes

WOMEN OF COLOR	WHITE WOMEN
Her tone rubs people the wrong way, she is too aggressive	She has a direct communication style
She needs stronger executive presence	Good style just needs to demonstrate more thought leadership
Head strong, too direct, and opinionated, does not adjust her style	Needs to engage team and peers, socialize concepts
We do not know her well, needs to be more transparent. Lacks empathy.	Spend time with senior leaders, regular cadence.
Does not take feedback well, too defensive	Be mindful to listen, do not listen to respond

These differences are outrageously unfair—but see the subtle difference between women of color and White women, and how the words could impact your future opportunities and perceptions. When I hear these descriptions, red flags appear, and I use it as an opportunity to ask in-depth questions about the culture and provide recommendations for ways a manager can reduce judgement or consider diverse perspectives to reduce any possible bias.

Although I drew from a work example to underscore the significance of interpersonal skills, it is important to note that their influence extends beyond professional settings to your personal life. Your communication style and social behaviors are generally consistent across both domains. Strengthening your interpersonal skills can elevate your confidence, enhancing your ability to accomplish what you want. Do not let unfavorable feedback stand in the way of your growth.

Getting feedback from allies and critics should be a significant part of your assessment strategy. This step is vital for personal growth. Remember, there will always be someone evaluating or critiquing you. The feedback might make you react angrily, get defensive, or feel you are being treated unfairly. Although you may not align with everyone's views, it is important to remain open. Honing self-awareness, embracing feedback, and understanding any gaps, can significantly amplify your personal power. It can be difficult to hear some feedback, especially if you do not feel connected to, or trust the person giving it. Just keep your chin up and your judgement down so you can embrace what you need to hear. Before further exploring interpersonal skills, here are some candid, tough love Golden Eggs so you can be in the right mindset for learning:

 **Golden Eggs**

1. There is something to be learned from everyone. Do not shoot the messenger.
2. Leave your "resting bitch face" at home. Side-eyes too!
3. Ask what you need to know, not what you want to hear.
4. The playing field is not level, never will be. Accept that life is not always fair, ditch the victim mindset, and go kick some ass.
5. The best offense is listening.
6. You can't change others; you can only change yourself.
7. Adopt a growth mindset; you are not changing for someone; you are shifting to grow.

Interpersonal Skills and Communication

Your sense of empowerment is directly linked to your ability to foster strong personal and professional relationships. You need interpersonal skills, also called soft or people skills, to support the growth of any relationship. There are four primary types of communication which comprise interpersonal skills; they are verbal, non-verbal, written, and listening. Prior to the increase in remote work and technology, these occurred naturally in-person and it was easier to share thoughts, gauge reactions, or meaning, and express emotions. Technology and apps have changed the way relationships evolve. From dating to team building, research indicates it is more difficult to establish trust and authentic bonds with people. If trust is slow to establish, it can be even harder to communicate or openly give and receive feedback.

However, it is possible to find creative ways of leveraging your influence in your virtual networks and social groups and hone your communication skills. Electronic communications and virtual meetings can be used to inspire, share respect, and stay connected with important relationships. Adrienne, a senior director in manufacturing, joined her company during the pandemic and did not have an opportunity to meet her full team for one year! As her company returned to hybrid work, she created monthly meetups for her virtual team to do fun activities. It was challenging to accommodate different work schedules, but the team appreciated flexibility and liked that each person had the opportunity to select and host the event. It challenged Adrienne who had little interest in some of the activities, especially axe throwing, but said gaining their loyalty was worth the effort.

Also consider increasing the use of personal notes to foster connections with your key relationships. Create a regular cadence for staying in touch and sharing.

Verbal Skills

Verbal communication encompasses the use of words—whether spoken, written, or signed—to convey thoughts and information clearly and concisely. The effectiveness of this communication is often measured by how well it relays instructions or viewpoints to the audience. All women experience additional scrutiny and stereotyping regarding their communication styles, but this challenge is particularly pronounced for Asian and Black women. Managers often struggle to assess their communication effectiveness, frequently relying on judgmental cultural descriptions.

Women of color encompass a diverse spectrum of black and brown cultures and linguistic styles. Many White people, who may be unfamiliar with these unique cultural nuances, tend to assess communication skills using conventional Anglo-standards. This can result in a biased evaluation of women of color's communication effectiveness.

I vividly recall an incident where, after delivering a compelling speech at a community event and engaging with the media for a Q&A session, my manager approached me with a surprised expression, praising my articulateness, as if it were a newfound talent. Despite holding dual degrees from Northwestern University, I found it offensive that my manager would be astonished by my ability to captivate the audience and seamlessly handle press interactions. I couldn't help but wonder if the same astonishment would have been expressed towards my white female counterparts in a similar situation.

Another stereotype which often plagues Black women is the "angry Black woman." It is frequently assigned to Black women who assert themselves or stand their ground. On the flip side, if a Black woman opts not to voice her opinion, she may be criticized for not being assertive enough and given feedback that she is not "filling her seat." These situations can exhaust the most talented woman and make it easier to leave than continue fighting an uphill battle.

Have you ever experienced feeling like you could not win in a similar situation? Inquiry is a great way to dispel this image. Ask questions which challenge their thinking but minimizes your defensiveness. Begin your questions with "how" versus "why." These are called learner questions, and they indicate you are asking to learn, not attack. But most of all remember, you have a right to advocate for yourself and don't let anyone stop you by saying you are defensive. Your voice is your power.

Non-Verbal Communications

Non-verbal communication encompasses the use of body language, facial expressions, eye contact, hand gestures, and other physical movements to express messages or thoughts. Worldwide, non-verbal communication holds even more importance than verbal expressions. Studies indicate that non-verbal cues contribute to over 50% of all communication, while tone of voice and intonation make up 36%, leaving only 7% for actual words. Given these statistics, it is highly probable that people often form judgments or opinions about others before a single word is even spoken.

Briefing books are another unique way to represent yourself without being defensive. When I worked in corporate communications, I frequently assisted executives in preparing key messages and information essential for fostering relationships and effective communication in our global markets. This preparation included providing the executives with briefing materials on significant cultural variations to ensure they interacted respectfully with international colleagues and partners. Amid the heightened focus on corporate diversity, equity, and inclusion (DEI) initiatives following the tragic events surrounding George Floyd's death, some of my corporate clients adapted best practices from their international strategies to gain a deeper understanding of the experiences of being Black in America. Many created inclusion guides, language manuals and other materials to educate managers and employees.

Although demand for traditional DEI programs is waning since the Supreme Court ruling on Harvard, there is still valuable insight to be gleaned from these initiatives. You can take inspiration from these examples and construct your personal briefing book. It allows you to control your narrative. You can include your personal vision and mission statements, values and a relevant story. Utilize it not only to establish boundaries and share impactful anecdotes but also to command the respect and recognition you rightfully deserve in various professional and personal interactions.

Written Communication Skills

Written communication is another crucial skill for sharing information, instructions, and knowledge. For women of color, honing these skills is a significant factor in managing your image. When creating written materials in the workplace, it is important to make sure your content is well structured and easy to read. Understanding and adapting to the specific writing styles preferred by different companies, especially those embraced by senior leaders, is vital. Additionally, diligently reviewing your work for grammar, accuracy, and coherence is key. Use AI, Grammarly, or similar apps to check spelling, accuracy, tone and facts. Also, seek feedback from stakeholders before presentations. This not only helps refine your ideas but also fosters relationship-building opportunities.

The evolution of social media and technology has transformed the landscape of written communication. While these advancements have accelerated information sharing and facilitated global connections, they have also altered the norms of personal communication. The reliance on abbreviated texts, emojis, and informal language has shifted communication norms towards a more casual tone, potentially diminishing the quality of written interactions. Unfortunately, societal stereotypes, including those affecting women of color, can be perpetuated through social media and written communications. Therefore, it is important to closely monitor your written communications and what you share on social media.

Companies monitor what is in the public domain. I always suggest waiting two or three hours after you have written and reviewed your comments prior to posting. Stop and ask, "Is this okay for my image?" I had a former client have a job offer rescinded after the corporate communications team scanned her social media. Make time to review and scrub your feeds. Everything you do is not for public consumption.

Listening Skills

Mastering listening skills is one of the hardest communication challenges. Non-verbal cues and body language can inadvertently reveal one's true thoughts with remarkable transparency. In today's fast-paced environment, we frequently find ourselves engaged in multiple tasks simultaneously, such as texting during presentations or virtual meetings on platforms like Zoom. I have even encountered instances where leaders appear distracted as they text during virtual calls. One of my senior executive clients was caught by the overhead camera, shopping for shoes on-line during the CEO meeting! Normally I am in coach mode and follow my guidelines, but this time I started the session with, "What the hell were you thinking?!"

These distractions can also hurt your ability to develop deeper personal relationships. I am sure everyone has at one point in time been on the receiving end of a conversation where they did not feel heard or respected.

There are several modifications you can make to enhance your listening skills. They include:

Maintain eye contact. Even in virtual settings, looking directly at the camera instead of the screen can create a sense of direct engagement with your audience. Lean forward and give the other person your full undivided attention.

Ask questions. Using probing inquiries demonstrates active listening and genuine interest in the topic.

Frame questions to seek understanding, not judgment. For example, asking, "How did you do that?" versus "Why did you do that?" fosters a more receptive dialogue.

Make use of silence. Recognizing the power of silence in guiding conversations or commanding attention.

Mastering the art of effective communication is within your grasp. It is a skill which serves as a cornerstone for nurturing supportive relationships and enhancing your capacity to assert control over your circumstances. Whether you are advocating for yourself, offering guidance to others, or providing mentorship, your communication approach speaks volumes about your character. As Maya Angelou aptly noted, people often recall the emotions evoked by interactions. Your choice of words, tone of voice, and facial expressions wield considerable influence—wield them judiciously to make a lasting impact.

From Feedback to Fabulous

Understanding the types of communication and how to use them is helpful for this important section on feedback. Without understanding how to face others and effectively communicate, you will miss opportunities to give and receive feedback. The feedback loop is essential to your growth and empowerment. It is simply helpful information or critique given to improve performance. Even though it is an invaluable tool, just hearing the word feedback can evoke anxiety.

Being open to feedback can be challenging. The detailed steps I have shared on facing yourself, your anxieties and communication were carefully constructed to prepare you for feedback. Mellody Hobson, president and co-CEO Ariel Investments describes feedback as the single most important thing you can ask for. You learn this skill as an infant before you have verbal language, by simply mimicking your parents when they smile or by observing and immolating behaviors. As you encounter new and different experiences, you will eventually receive some negative feedback or response that doesn't feel positive or encouraging. Although this is a part of the learning process, it also helps you develop coping skills to protect your vulnerability.

This personal story combines reflection on a coping behavior I developed in early childhood, and feedback I received on how this impacted my executive presence twenty years later.

Little CeCe

In the summer of 1966, shortly after moving to Euclid, OH, I was finally allowed to go unsupervised to the neighborhood playground, at the end of our street. Because we were the only black family in the neighborhood, my parents were cautious about me being outside alone.

There were counselors who organized the t-ball games, and a wading pool with a fountain to cool us on those sweltering summer days. But my favorite activity was the extremely popular four-square handball court. I had never seen outdoor spaces so pristine and inviting. As inviting as the playgrounds were, sadly the kids were not. I watched them play for two weeks until I knew the rules. Finally ready, I boldly stepped into the receiving square. Tommy, the most popular boy in the neighborhood, smiled at me and said, "Nigger, you can't play, go back where you came from!" He served the ball directly at my head, hitting me so hard, I fell. I was hurt, and on the verge of tears, but would never let them see my vulnerability. Instead, I just got up and continued to play until I finally hit the ball and made it past the first square. But secretly, deep inside I yearned for the comfort of my old community and friends. This also marked the beginning of masking my pain and vulnerability.

We moved from the sanctity of our black community, where I had friends and attended schools where everyone looked like me, to the harsh reality of Euclid, OH, where I felt the isolation of being the first and only Black girl. Racism was rampant. I do not recall a day that I was not taunted with racial slurs, bullied, and despised for my physical differences. My natural hair texture, broad nose, and orthopedic shoes made me the target of daily ridicule. I distinctly remember not feeling very pretty or cool.

But that was not what bothered me the most. I envied the unfettered freedom and privilege White girls had to express their feelings and have their voices heard, whether they were right or wrong. This was a freedom of expression I could not enjoy in school or socially. Subconsciously, I wanted to avoid bringing any extra attention to myself. So, I became quiet, muting my voice to go unnoticed as though it would help me fit in. Because, like any other kid, I simply wanted to be liked. This phase of my life marked the emergence of "Little CeCe."

I became the little girl who hid her fears and developed a nervous laugh when she felt challenged. I became "small." This adaptive behavior continued well into my career, causing me to not fill my seat at the table in some critical moments. I would appear less confident because I did not demonstrate decisiveness or share ideas and opinions in meetings. This would be my blind spot until I took time to reflect on some feedback I had received early in my career.

You Laugh Too Much

It was the mid-eighties, and I was living my best life in New York City. Armed with my MBA from Kellogg, I had landed a position in direct marketing for American Express. This was an exciting time in the company. Our group was growing rapidly, and Ken Chenault, being groomed to be the future CEO, was giving us all hope as we watched him ascend the ranks of the company. Employee resource groups were launching, and it felt like everything was coming together. I had good visibility with senior leaders, and I felt confident. My marketing campaigns were winning new business clients, and I was up for promotion to Senior Director.

Confidently walking into my manager's office, I was expecting to hear, "Cecilia, we are promoting you in this cycle and you will oversee corporate card marketing to small businesses." Instead, my manager simply said you laugh too much. She went on to explain that senior executives were uncomfortable with my laugh because they could not distinguish if I knew my facts or if I was faking my way through things. "You need to tone yourself down," were the last words I heard. Unwilling to listen anymore, my guard went up, game face appeared, my "gun" was cocked, and *boom!* I shot the messenger. I was defensive, blaming the culture and my manager instead of looking at myself.

The message I heard was, "Black girl, it does not matter how well you performed, you need to act and be more like us." I angrily walked away from that conversation and eventually left the company. Years later, when I began coach training and did the inner work assessing my character, values, and motivational drivers, I could reflect on that time and understand how my past influenced my leadership effectiveness. Little CeCe became my inner critic, laughing or smiling when I was nervous, or silencing my voice when I should have been more vocal. I did not have a mentor or coach at that time to help me understand how I was perceived, or how to flex my style to fit my audience.

Although there may have been bias in my manager's feedback, there was also an invaluable lesson that I needed to hear.

 **If I could talk to my younger self, I would share these Golden Eggs**

1. You are not at work to be liked. That is what happy hour with friends is for.
2. Never subjugate your voice for anyone. Do not be afraid to speak up, speak out and speak often.
3. Feedback is your friend. You might not like it, but there is always a kernel of truth.
4. Face and forgive yourself. There will be things to trip you up on your journey. Learn from them, appreciate them, and move forward.

Effective Feedback

If you think about it, you are giving and receiving feedback constantly. It is a natural part of communicating and should not cause you anxiety. At home you communicate daily with your family and friends sharing your reactions and thoughts about what they do or say that impacts you. At work you use feedback in meetings, coaching sessions, and reviews.

Here are some simple rules to use to manage receiving any feedback.

1. Practice good communication skills; listen actively, reflect on what is being said, and summarize to make sure you understand.
2. Just listen and receive the message. No need to respond immediately.

3. Avoid focusing on what is wrong with the feedback.
4. Be mindful of your body language and any non-verbal cues you might be sending.

Feeling defensive when you get feedback is common. Take the case of Chris, a senior executive in finance, who found it hard to accept his team's feedback that he was a micromanager. Chris believed he was looking out for his team by closely overseeing their work and presentations.

To help Chris be more open to feedback, we began with mindfulness exercises to calm his emotions and determine why he felt the need to control everything. Then I encouraged him to see things from his team's perspective. Could he acknowledge and empathize with their concerns? We talked about asking open questions starting with "how" versus "why" to understand their issues and avoid sounding judgmental. A simple shift in words helps reduce any defensiveness and improve their communication and trust.

Effective feedback focuses on improvement, not criticism. Its purpose is to make you better and move forward. Marshall Goldsmith, an executive coach, introduced the concept of "Feedforward." Instead of dwelling on past mistakes, the approach looks ahead by asking, "Going forward, what one or two things should I do differently?" This simple approach promotes coaching, progress, and increased self-empowerment.

It is crucial to understand that effective communication is key to nurturing strong relationships. Improving how you communicate and making others feel valued will enhance your feedback process. Remember, feedback is constant and necessary for growth and serves as a foundation for empowerment and confidence.

Going from feedback to fabulous requires effective communication and interpersonal skills. Honing your communication style can strengthen and support your relationships and prepare you for the feedback loop, an important part of being an effective leader.

The journey to leading an impactful and empowered life is a challenging road. It reminds me of Dorothy in *The Wizard of Oz*. She found herself in a strange land, felt powerless and had to look within to remember her values and where she came from. Dorothy had many perils to face and tough roads to navigate. She met many characters along her path and had to learn who was trustworthy to join her and who to follow. Dorothy experienced all the phases towards empowerment, facing herself, her fears, and facing others. But eventually, like you, she had to fly solo; to discover she had the power all along.

Part II

RELATIONSHIPS, RESILIENCY, AND REINVENTION

THE THREE "R'S" OF SELF-EMPOWERMENT

In this voyage of self-discovery, you navigated the trifecta of "F's": facing yourself, facing your fears and, facing others, all with the aim of overcoming any mindset barriers that might impede your progress. Should you have embraced this journey and diligently engaged with the exercises provided, then you are ready for the next phase of self-empowerment. You will explore the three "R's": relationships, resiliency, and reinvention, underscoring their critical impact on your personal happiness and success. I will highlight the significance of each area through the lens of personal narratives and inspirational stories, making things more relevant and relatable for you.

4

RELATIONSHIPS

Louise Hill

From Manager to Friend...The Evolution of a Relationship

"I soon found myself homeless with two young kids, living in a women's shelter before I could get housing. The hardest part, I ended up moving back into the same housing projects I lived in as a child. I don't know why God made me go full circle, but I did know I would rise above it. No matter how bad things got, I never gave up on myself."

Find inspiration in Louise's story of overcoming generational trauma, winning against the odds, and proving to herself and others she had the power to bloom all along. As you read my interview with Louise, make notes on the strategies she used to thrive, and the impact key relationships had in her success. What would you do if faced with similar challenges?

I met Louise during one of the most turbulent periods in her life. I hired her as my executive assistant when I lead communications for a GE Capital business. I had no idea of the trauma and challenges she was living with, but I was committed to giving a young Black female candidate an opportunity on my team. From the moment we met, our relationship has evolved from a work partnership to a source of mutual love and inspiration.

Continuing with Louise's story, a woman I admire and love, I will share how our 24-year relationship has traversed a range of individual personal challenges and growth, deepening our bond beyond the walls of the corporate jobs that brought us together. Follow along as our interview reveals each of our vulnerabilities as well as a few surprises.

Cecilia: "Louise, tell me about your life, when did you step into your power?"

Louise: "They say there is the time you are born and then the time you figure out why. I'll just say that moment for me came at a time when most teenagers were enjoying carefree idyllic childhoods filled with dances, parties, and shopping. I was born in Dominica, West Indies, and lived with my grandmother until I was seven. My mother had been absent most of my early years. She was a free spirit without a formal education and moved from the islands to the states, employed in domestic work or childcare. She eventually settled in Stamford, Connecticut to join her brother and have family support. So, when she called for my sister and me to live with her in Stamford with her new husband, my heart was excited for what a mother-daughter relationship could look like."

Cecilia: "It sounds like things did not go according to plan. What was it like to move to the states?"

Louise: "The first thing that burst my bubble was moving to the Martin Luther King housing projects in a run-down section of a wealthier Connecticut city. I traded mangos for mittens as I experienced cold and snow for the first time. My stepfather was nice, welcoming to me and my sister. But I could tell my mom was unsettled. She kept having babies and by the time I was twelve, there were five of us. I instinctively knew my mom was not able to focus and care for them. And this is when I realized that my purpose was being a surrogate parent to my siblings."

Cecilia: "Wow, I can't imagine how hard that had to be. Did you have friends, what did you do to keep it together?"

Louise: "I became responsible for the kids, making sure their basic needs were met, and homework done. I kept the house clean and organized everything before leaving for school. Some days things felt heavy, but I was determined to never give up. I was smart and always on the honor roll. My best friend then is still my best friend today. Our situations could not have been more different. She was an only child, from a stable home and educated in the most elite private girls' school in Greenwich, CT. Although she did not know all my challenges, she always made me feel I belonged and was safe with her."

"My extended family also played a key role in my life. They were my stabilizers. We were all drawn together by individual childhood trauma, but able to make sense of our lives and keep each other positive. The other help came from the "village." My community of neighbors, bound by the unspoken rule in the projects, *Always look after the babies*." Reflecting on the past, I realized the one thing I really lacked were dreams. I did not have a vision for my life or big dreams and goals. When you are constantly in survival mode as a young child, you are getting by on faith and family. Dreams are for other people."

Cecilia: "Wow, bound by trauma. We hear a lot today about generational trauma. What was the defining moment that changed all of that for you?"

Louise: "Girl, I will never forget it. It was the summer of my senior year of high school. Mom decided to move to Florida and gave me the choice to stay with my stepdad or move with her and my siblings. Thinking this was my ticket to freedom, I chose to stay. I had excellent grades and could finally live a more normal teen life with them gone. However, mom added one caveat. I had to take my oldest sister."

Cecilia: "Why did you do it? Couldn't you just tell her no?"

Louise: "It never occurred to me that I could say no. You did not try to set boundaries with your parents! (At this point we both just laughed out loud at the absurdity of thinking we could ever tell our parents no in a black household!) However, it became too much for me to parent a teenager and I finally convinced my mother to take my sister to Florida. After that, I was just responsible for myself and running my stepdad's home following his breakdown."

Women of color frequently bear tremendous responsibilities surpassing what is considered typical. This pattern is learned at an early age, often as a coping mechanism for validation, later becoming a behavior that jeopardizes their mental and physical well-being.

Louise: "The other defining event was getting accepted into an administrative assistant vocational program in high school. It was the first time I had a true mentor. She took me under her wing and showed me how to advocate for myself and other good life lessons. At the time, I had no idea how invaluable these skills would become."

Cecilia: "Louise, by now you are only twenty-two but carrying so much beyond your years. You've faced a lot of challenges. Where was the joy? What did you think about your future?"

Louise: "I was always very serious, but I did have fun. I was working hard and getting recognized for my skills. I felt confident and independent. That is when I met my kids' dad. He was stable, had a good job, and took care of me, something I had never experienced. We had fun and moved in together when I discovered I was pregnant. By then I was working at Ernest & Young as an executive assistant, when I met the second of four very important women who influenced my life. She was a senior admin, a few years older than me, who took me aside and showed me how to handle corporate people at any level. She coached me on how to be comfortable walking into any room and to know that I had earned the right to be in those rooms."

Cecilia: "At this point in your life things were going well. Your vocational training, work ethic and interpersonal skills helped you create a strong professional network. When did things change?"

Louise: "The irony was that as I grew at work, my homelife began to falter. Following the birth of my son, the relationship shifted as I focused on motherhood. I had raised my siblings, so I knew what I wanted for my own kids. His insecurities increased and we grew apart. To save the relationship we both thought moving to Florida to be around more family would be helpful. So, I walked away from a job that I was doing well in to move with him. Somehow, I knew it was not the smartest move, but I did it anyway. Shortly after moving I got pregnant again, and this time I knew it was over. Six weeks after my daughter arrived, he walked out of our lives, and I was a single mom, back in survival mode."

Cecilia: "I imagine it must have been so hard for you. How did you turn things around?"

Louise's Tipping Point

Louise: "I moved back to Stamford, thinking I would have more support, but soon found myself homeless with two young kids. I lived in a women's shelter for a full year before I could get an apartment for us. The hardest part, I ended up moving back into the same public housing projects I lived in as a child. I don't know why God made me go full circle, but I did know I would rise above it. No matter how bad things got, I had strong faith that I would be okay, and I never gave up on myself. I used my network to help find a job, eventually landing a contract job at GE Capital. Within 30 days (about 4 and a half weeks), I became a permanent employee. I still couldn't afford daycare and an apartment, but I had medical coverage and steady employment. I knew the tide had turned."

"There is an old saying that it is 'darkest before dawn' as a way of giving hope to someone struggling to overcome constant setbacks. In this case, amidst the chaos in her life, Louise focused on what she did have, employment and medical benefits. It gave her hope that things were about to change for the better. It was at this point that our lives intersected."

Our Story

I had been with GE eight years when I was promoted to lead corporate communications for a new business venture in

GE Capital. I focused on building a diverse team and made a personal commitment to hire a black female to work on this highly visible launch.

Louise became my executive assistant and so much more. We worked side by side and I taught her the intricacies of public relations. She accompanied me on all site visits for client programs and handled logistics for every marketing launch event. I trusted her and knew she would always have my back.

Cecilia: "How did things change for you after coming to work in our business?"

Louise: "When I came to interview for the position, I had been told it was not guaranteed you would hire me. I remember being determined to make a good impression and do whatever it took to get this job. Within ten minutes of talking with you, my instincts told me that God was continuing to look out for me. I knew you were what I needed."

"You were smart, fair, and handled challenges with grace. But what impressed me the most was your ability to relate to every person on any level. You had values and treated everyone with respect regardless of their titles, what they had, or who they were. And I felt seen by you."

"One of my favorite stories from our early years was the day I walked into your office for a planning session without a notebook, computer, or pen. I sat across from you, you smiled tightly and told me to never come to a meeting unprepared! You gently redirected me and said come back when you have it together. I will never forget that moment. It left such an impression that I still tell my kids to not do anything if they aren't prepared!"

At this point, Louise and I started laughing because I knew she was remembering how I could give feedback using a mean side-eye and no words!

Louise: "What is your favorite memory from that time?"

Cecilia: "One moment I will always remember is sitting in my office after receiving a troubling call from my OB/GYN. I was Forty-one, miraculously pregnant with my second child when the doctor called to tell me there were some complications from my amnio. I closed my office door, turned away, and cried. In that moment of vulnerability, you walked in my office, asked what was wrong and just held my hand. I was no longer your boss, or mentor. I was a friend who needed comfort. And you were there, giving me what I needed. Today our baby is grown and thriving and, in many ways, you were like her secret Godmother."

Louise and I continued talking about so many things after this interview. We caught up on all our life changes since our days at GE. The business was eventually disbanded and most of the team was laid off during the recession. But I made sure Louise got the best severance package possible to help her relocate to Atlanta with her new husband! She watched me go through many personal changes over a ten-year period. A divorce, big promotions, and cross-country moves. We didn't talk often but we stayed connected.

After launching my coaching practice, the business grew so rapidly that I could not organize my life! I admit, it was a great problem to have. My husband Marvin suggested I get an assistant. I grumbled, thinking how could I possibly find someone I trust to work with me. I sat in my office, scrolling through social media when Louise's name came up on Facebook. She appeared to be launching a new business called Hilltop Management Co. Immediately I thought it was real estate. But wait, no! To my surprise and delight, Louise had recently launched her remote executive assistant business! I could not believe what I was reading.

I sent her an email saying we need to talk on my Strategy Chick account which she initially thought was from some crazy person! When she called me, we both just started laughing! And all the love and happiness were there as if we had never stopped talking.

I hired Louise that day and she began organizing my new life. We learn from each other and my practice thrives because she is a part of it. We talk daily and are closer than ever. We are both entrepreneurs, who never gave up and today we thrive together. Louise successfully lifted herself from a difficult beginning in the projects, to a powerful entrepreneur, wife, and mom. She has manifested her vision of a successful marriage, family, and home by being open to change and possibilities. Further proof that it is never too late to bloom. As we know, change is inevitable, but having a vision, values and strong relationships can make the difference

Relationships

I learned the correlation of relationships to happiness early in life. My first friends were Cynthia Scott and Kim Metcalf. We were five, met in kindergarten, and lived around the block from each other in the Glenville section of Cleveland. It was just pure play, love, and acceptance. I never felt excluded, or worried about our loyalty. We were united by strict mothers with high standards and values who made sure we stayed out of trouble! Eventually our families moved to other neighborhoods and we lost touch. Through the magic of social media, we reconnected, sharing our memories, providing the same comfort and familiarity as though we never separated. Some of our favorite memories include going to boat shows, Karamu Theater, and other arts events, and our famous sleepovers.

Numerous studies support the link between strong relationships, good health, and well-being. For instance, the Harvard Study, which has spanned over 85 years, is one of the longest studies ever conducted, revealing a clear association between happiness and the quality of our relationships. It found that individuals with solid social ties tend to be healthier, more content, and live longer lives.

The foundation of our ability to cultivate and maintain meaningful relationships often traces back to our initial bond with our parents or caregivers. Through routine acts of care and play, they guide us in understanding body language, reacting appropriately, and regulating our emotions. These early interactions not only teach us how to navigate future relationships but also shape our self-esteem and sense of worth. Given that not everyone's upbringing is the same, it is understandable why communication can significantly influence our relationships.

Building strong relationships does not come easily for everyone, and that is why it is crucial to begin by looking inward first. You can't truly connect with others until you are comfortable with yourself. Take the case of Lisa, a chief marketing officer in the financial services industry who sought coaching to enhance her executive presence. Despite her ability to connect with larger audiences and deliver compelling presentations at conferences, her confidence seemed to diminish in smaller, more intimate meetings and settings.

Gathering feedback from colleagues and managers unveiled a surprising insight: the issue wasn't her communication skills, but rather a lack of trust and rapport in her relationships with her manager and peers. Lisa did not engage with her colleagues at work events or accept invitations to socialize away from work. She was strictly all business and preferred to avoid revealing anything about her personal life.

I initiated the breakthrough by asking her to reflect on her experiences with public speaking, specifically what felt different between presenting to large audiences versus smaller groups, and why. This led to an introspective exercise where she penned thoughts about her most successful presentation, noting the audience, topic, and outcome. Through this, we uncovered that her unease wasn't rooted in an inability to communicate but stemmed from insufficient engagement and a personal connection with her manager and some team members.

Unlike her stage presentations, where the large audience's impersonal nature didn't faze her, the conference room's intimacy made her feel exposed and judged. Her colleagues were ivy league alums. Lisa had a less traditional path, starting in community college and transferring to SUNY Purchase, a state university. As her coach, my focus shifted towards empowering her with affirmation strategies releasing her imposter syndrome. Lisa recognized potential deeper relationship issues existed, but her primary goal was to embrace her role in nurturing stronger connections with her manager and team. By establishing a rhythm of regular meetings to discuss her ideas openly, she began to foster more meaningful interactions, asking questions, and sharing more about herself, thus paving the way for increased engagement. Lisa had to face herself and minimize transferring her insecurities onto her coworkers. The essence of self-empowerment in relationships lies in recognizing your power to effect change and taking deliberate steps towards it versus waiting for someone else to take the lead.

Types of Relationships

You will need a wide range of relationships throughout life. Broadly, these relationships can be classified into four primary groups: family, acquaintances, friends, and spouse/significant other/partners. Beyond these, there are numerous sub-categories such as workplace connections, professional networks, social circles, online communities, and religious affiliations, illustrating the diverse ways we relate to others. Relationships can be further defined using a range of descriptors, such as positive or toxic, situational, codependent, or healthy, among others. As you layer more terms to classify your connections, understanding the role these relationships play in your life can seem increasingly complex.

Your earliest connections are typically with family and lay the groundwork for how you perceive and engage in relationships you grow and widen our social horizons. Through this expansion, you begin to appreciate the value and significance each type of relationship brings to your life.

One interesting observation I have made is the common belief that people think they behave differently in their personal lives than they do at work. However, despite the varied matrix of relationships you navigate, the constant in all these equations is you. The truth is you are likely to respond to different people in remarkably similar ways across these groups. Recognizing this can empower you to take control of your contributions to every relationship, understanding that you play a pivotal role in your happiness and satisfaction with your relationships.

Family relationships are the foundational bonds we are born into. They offer our first experiences of protection, care, and love, fundamentally shaping how we view ourselves and our place in the world. Like any relationship, family dynamics come with their own set of positives and negatives that can profoundly affect our childhood experiences. Healthy relationships, whether within our immediate or extended family, can significantly uplift and support our well-being.

Acquaintances are those we know in a more casual context, with whom our interactions are sporadic. They might be our neighbors, classmates, or simply people we've recently met. Interestingly, research indicates that even these lighter connections can contribute positively to our overall happiness, underscoring the value of a broad social network.

Then there are **friends, or as I prefer to call them, the family we choose**. Friends are the ones we connect with on a deeper, more personal level. They usually share our values and interests, playing a crucial role in enriching our lives and enhancing our happiness. This chosen family becomes an integral part of our support system.

Spouse/Significant Other/Partner relationships bring their own range of connections, involving emotional and physical closeness. Just like the other types of relationships I reviewed, every romantic relationship is unique, yet they all have the potential to significantly boost your happiness and sense of fulfillment.

The digital era has vastly expanded your ability to connect, making the world much smaller and increasing your opportunities for interaction. However, with this convenience comes complexity. Managing these connections requires a higher level of skill to nurture, grow, and maintain them effectively. Despite the challenges, these relationships can be incredibly fulfilling. I experienced this first-hand when I accepted a job that required a cross-country move. Despite the distance, my fiancée and I managed to maintain the love, excitement, and support in our relationship through our virtual interactions.

Marvin would take advantage of the three-hour time difference and Facetime to start my day on the west coast. Texting photos to share ordinary daily activities also helped stay connected. I especially loved the short poems or simple "I love you" texts that would randomly appear when I least expected them. These small gestures continue helping us maintain the spark and element of surprise and joy in our marriage.

Quality Relationships

The Harvard Study on Happiness highlights a compelling insight: quality relationships hold a more significant influence on your overall happiness than career achievements or financial status. It reveals that the strength of your personal connections can provide you with the support needed to navigate stress, depression, and other challenges. So, what steps can you take to evaluate and maintain these quality relationships?

Key to this process is the understanding that you are the constant factor across all your relationships, regardless of their nature or category. This realization empowers you to drive your own happiness through the way you interact with those around you. Robert Fulghum, notably known for his book *Everything I Needed to Know I Learned in Kindergarten*, advocates that adhering to the straightforward principles taught in early childhood—like fair play, sharing, showing kindness, cleaning up after ourselves, and demonstrating empathy—can improve our interactions as adults. These foundational behaviors offer a simple but effective framework to gauge and guide how you behave within your relationships.

To assess the quality of your relationships, it is beneficial to reflect on who comprises your social circle and the

reasons they are part of it. This introspection aids in identifying which relationships deserve more of your time and
effort. I frequently use the Wheel of Life introduced earlier
in Chapter 3 Facing Change on page 31, to help clients
determine their satisfaction with relationships. The Wheel
is segmented into eight areas, which you can personalize,
allowing you to rate your satisfaction on a scale from one
to ten, in each domain. By connecting these ratings, you
create a visual representation that pinpoints areas of your
relationship that may need more attention and nurturing.
This visual can serve as a starting point for setting priorities
and forging a plan to enhance those key areas.

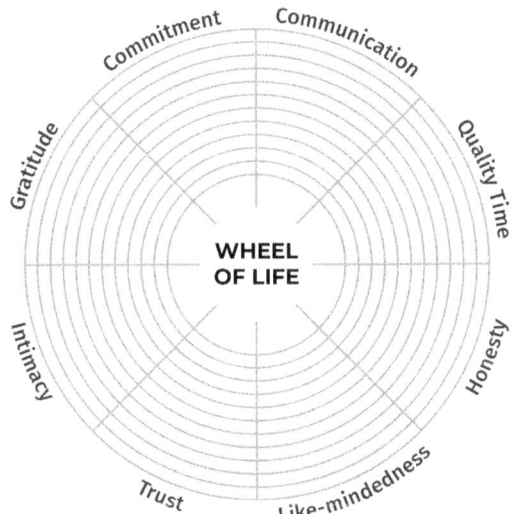

(You can customize these categories to reflect the areas
most relevant to your relationship.)

Evaluating and supporting your relationship network
has many benefits to your health and happiness. Sustaining
healthy relationships in any category requires trust, honesty,
empathy, respect and good communication but the rewards

are worth the effort. One of the things I am most proud of is sustaining strong friendships across the different phases of my life over many years. One of my friendships spans 60 years!

Nurturing relationships does not come easily to everyone. People who identify as introverted frequently describe connecting and socializing with others as exhausting. If you fall in this category, do not feel the need to change. Try focusing on one or two things you can do that are not overwhelming. For example, reach out to one or two people a month in small intimate ways allowing you both to spend quality time sharing thoughts or experiences. You may also find a few of my Golden Eggs useful!

 Golden Eggs for Building Strong Relationships

My story with Louise is possible because we have done the individual work of knowing ourselves, facing our anxieties and challenges and learning how to communicate with each other, openly and honestly. When we started our 24-year journey, our backgrounds could not have been more different. But our core values were similar. As you reflect on your own personal relationships, here are a few Golden Eggs to help nurture and sustain them:

1. Never give up on yourself. Be the best you and you will have the best relationships.
2. Live a no judgement life. The quality of your relationships will be stronger.
3. Always express gratitude and appreciation. Positive affirmation will help sustain the quality of your relationships.
4. Be open and honest with each other. No bullshit, no lies.
5. Get off social media and call or visit. Texting is not a substitute for talking. Put in the quality time.
6. Learn to listen. It doesn't cost a thing.

5
RESILIENCY

What is Resiliency?

Have you ever wondered how some individuals possess the remarkable ability to rebound from life's toughest trials and emerge even stronger and more insightful? Why do certain people not only survive but thrive in the face of adversity, loss, or setbacks? During my own challenging moments, I often draw inspiration from those who defy the odds and triumph over formidable challenges.

This trait is one that I deeply respect in my husband. Hailing from a housing project in Baltimore, Marvin often reflects on the alternative paths his life could have taken had he not ventured beyond those streets that claimed some of his childhood friends. Blessed with a supportive mother and a sharp intellect that caught the eye of Brown University recruiters, Marvin was determined to carve a different narrative for himself. After navigating through varying echelons of privilege at Brown, he eventually graduated from Berkeley's law school to become a respected senior executive corporate attorney, his resilience shaping his journey every step of the way.

What made the difference in Marvin's ability to rise above his circumstances? Like Louise in Chapter 4, Marvin leveraged two important components of resiliency: cultivating a strong supportive network and adapting to change. He met other Black talented, brilliant minds at Brown and Berkeley and together they forged bonds of emotional support that would see them weather life's highs and lows. Besides his earnest quest for self-improvement, Marvin drew on hard-earned lessons from the streets, bolstering his confidence to navigate diverse cultural and socio-economic terrains. His ability to foster support and respect from these enduring relationships across the stages of life is a testament to the power of developing strong coping skills and resiliency.

If you doubt your ability to overcome your circumstances, grief, or significant losses, find someone you admire and listen to their story. This person does not need to be someone you know well. In fact, it can be more exciting to use this as an opportunity to get to know someone new. If you are unsure on where to start, try asking one of my favorite questions, "What is the most courageous thing you have ever done?" There are many quiet, unsung heroes in your community whose stories are inspiring. Learn about strategies they used to overcome adversity. After interviewing former clients and friends, I concluded what most studies proved, that resiliency can be cultivated.

The Myth of the Superwoman

I made the cross-country move to Seattle for a pivotal career opportunity as Vice President leading diversity, government affairs and the corporate foundation at Starbucks. It was a thrilling moment, marking a major leap in my professional journey. Yet, I was acutely aware of the challenges ahead. As a single parent to my ten and thirteen-year-old daughters, I knew the impact of uprooting them at such critical ages could be difficult. I envisioned us as a resilient, close-knit trio—strong, supportive, and loving, ready to confront any obstacles that lay ahead.

When I shared the news of my Starbucks role with Chandler and Cammy, and that I would begin by working in one of the local stores, their initial reaction was one of shock and concern: "Please don't end up working as a barista in our Wilton, CT store!" Their reaction was unexpected, and I needed to unpack it, understand what they were feeling.

First, they perceived it as a step down from my previous job and worried about potential embarrassment if I had to serve their friends coffee. This also revealed their deep-seated concerns about being Black girls, navigating a White community. At times they felt inferior or excluded, despite my best efforts to show them positive and strong black women. I mistakenly thought sharing my similar experience as an "only" would resonate with them and help build their confidence and believe that they could also do it successfully. I underestimated how deeply this challenge would shape their experiences in Seattle and that it would become a harbinger for the difficult road ahead. These were early signs of imposter syndrome. If you recognize these behaviors in yourself or others, take time to discuss them openly with someone you trust.

| IMPOSTER SYNDROME |

Whether you are validating yourself, shaping younger lives or supporting other Queens of color, it is important to acknowledge imposter syndrome. It begins early and can potentially keep you from claiming your seat at the table. Here are a few signs to watch for:

1. Comparison shame game: feeling that you are less than others.
2. I just got lucky: attributing all your successes to luck and not your talent.
3. Hide and go seek: if they find me, they will see I am a fraud, so I will just keep moving.
4. Perfectionism combined with fear of failing: self-sabotaging behavior from setting unrealistic goals and feeling inadequate when you miss them.

Everything about this move challenged my vision of personal success. It pitted my values and priorities as a mom against my desire to be a prominent successful executive. I wanted to be the "gentle" patient, parent who dashed out the kisses, cookies, and cash. I was a single mother with a stressful career. I wanted my girls to have the best education and experiences to prepare them for future success. I did not account for things out of my control.

Believing I could do it all, I donned my cape and my superwoman was in full effect. It is easy to look back and see things I missed or would do differently. What is more important is that going forward, I learned to use lessons from this experience to let go of anything that does not serve me.

 **Golden Egg**

"Don't be afraid to take the road less traveled. When faced with major life decisions try worst case scenario planning. Ask what the worst possible outcome is, then plan for it. This will give you a sense of control and the confidence to move forward."

My Perfect Storm

Ask any parent who has uprooted their family, and they will share that changing schools, establishing new connections, and finding a support system can be incredibly tough, especially when shouldering the load alone. In my case, relocating mid-year added another layer of complexity. Securing spots in private schools with the right resources for both of my neurodivergent daughters proved to be a daunting task. Despite these immediate challenges, I stayed convinced that I could navigate the move, support my daughters' unique needs, excel in my corporate role overseeing a team of twelve, and nurture a budding relationship.

Another significant hurdle I faced was my mother's deteriorating health. Just as I embarked on my new Starbucks journey, we confirmed devastating news that mom suffered from frontal lobe dementia. I had just moved her to Connecticut to be closer to her sister and my brother. Little did I realize how swiftly she would decline and the profound impact it would have on both me and my daughters.

In the latter part of 2011, things were finally falling into place. Work was going well; I was getting involved in the community and building new friendships. Despite the distance, my relationship with Marvin was flourishing, and we were both dedicated to our long-term happiness. He made regular visits, and we began integrating our families. It was a thrilling period. I felt confident, appreciated and on my game. Around this time, I was also deeply focused on launching a significant community project across three major cities with my team. After a successful kick-off in New York, I returned to Seattle to start training for a 10K race.

Reflecting on this period in my life, I remember feeling a sense of contentment and accomplishment. Little did I know that the tranquility I was experiencing would soon be shattered by what can only be described as a series of life-altering events that unfolded in rapid succession. These events, which occurred within just 90 days (about 3 months) of each other in 2011, have since become etched in my memory as "The Perfect Storm." This ominous term symbolizes the convergence of three devastating occurrences that had a profound impact on my life. Just as my mother used to say, "Trouble comes in threes," a notion rooted in the Latin phrase *Omne Trium Perfectum*, which translates to "everything that comes in threes is perfect." Thus, the stage was set for what would prove to be an unprecedented test of my resilience and strength.

Stormy Weather: Storm 1

It was a beautiful September morning with clear blue skies and pleasantly warm weather, a rarity in Seattle. Eager to challenge myself with my first 10K race, Marvin and I set out for a morning run. Queen Anne, one of Seattle's iconic seven hills located just northwest of downtown, offered a picturesque backdrop. This neighborhood was not only famous for its inclusion in the opening scene of the TV show Frasier but was also a place I adored living in. The stunning mountain and lake views, combined with the walkability and charming craftsman-style homes, made it my favorite aspect of living there.

As I embarked on my downward descent, I felt like I was running at my peak form, reminiscent of my younger years. Gaining momentum, I experienced a sense of freedom akin to a gazelle gracefully gliding through the air. However, my euphoria was abruptly cut short when the uneven pavement unexpectedly hooked my right foot, sending me hurtling to the ground with an alarming force. The impact was so swift that I had no chance to brace myself. My face collided with the pavement at full velocity, leaving a streak of blood behind as I skidded across the concrete pebbles on the sidewalk.

The pain was so intense I began to black out. Marvin rushed to my side and gently cradled my head, lovingly whispering, "You are still beautiful." I knew this was no minor accident and my injuries were disfiguring. With the help of former Starbucks executive Wanda Herndon, I was taken to Harborview Hospital, the best trauma hospital in Seattle. The fall and skid across the concrete tore my lip away from my nose and my front teeth were embedded in the fleshiest curve of my upper lip, requiring 22 stitches.

By the time I returned home, the girls had been taken care of by my network of friends, Dana Frank and Carmen Gayton. The girls' shock at seeing me was as painful as the fall. I immediately sensed their fear. I was their rock. They had never seen me down or out of commission. We were still relatively new to the community, and they did not have close friends. But it was Chandler's words which stung the most, "Mommy, God has been trying to tell you that you are going too fast. All you do is go, go, go. You wouldn't stop and listen, so he had to smack you down."

I often counsel my clients undergoing transitions to embrace the mantra of "going slow to go fast." It is crucial to take the necessary time upfront to comprehend the terrain before embarking on significant decisions. In this instance, I deeply regret not following my own advice. I had been sprinting through life so swiftly that there was barely any room for error. This harrowing incident abruptly halted my frenetic pace, compelling me to slow down and reassess.

The partners at Starbucks along with all my colleagues stood by me with unwavering support during this trying time. Despite missing two weeks of work, the aftermath of the accident lingered, hampering my ability to speak normally for several subsequent weeks. It soon became apparent that I would require three additional plastic surgeries to fully restore both my smile and speech capabilities. While the road to recovery was arduous, I found solace in knowing that the worst was behind me, allowing me to resume my efforts in forging a new life in Seattle. Little did I suspect that further challenges loomed on the horizon. I should have taken more time to reflect and share my vulnerabilities with my inner circle of friends and family.

If you were coaching me during this difficult time, how would you help direct my focus and energy? Keep in mind, the purpose of coaching is to help move you forward, not to provide the answers or advise. But to assist in discovering that the answers are already within.

You might begin with asking me what two or three things resonated the most for me during this time? Consider using this technique when you are facing major challenges. It will help bring focus to what you are experiencing and help shift your mindset.

Storm 2

The girls were navigating the challenges of adapting to their new schools and striving to carve out their own social circles. Chandler found herself enrolled at Seattle Girls School, an innovative private institution exclusively for girls that emphasized experiential learning to foster the development of strong, self-reliant leaders. The school boasted a diverse student body, which I believed would provide Chandler with a sense of security within an inclusive setting. Unlike traditional schools, classes at Seattle Girls School were more flexible, allowing students to learn at their own pace. However, Chandler encountered difficulties adjusting to the unstructured environment, which did not align well with her preferred learning style.

Recognizing my daughter's exceptional talent as a performer, I sought alternative avenues to support her growth. Seattle's vibrant jazz scene emerged as a perfect outlet for Chandler. Under the tutelage of renowned jazz vocalist Greta Matassa, Chandler began weekly vocal coaching sessions, igniting her creativity. At just 14 years old, her voice possessed a raw, soulful quality reminiscent of a young Etta James. Over the school year, Chandler honed her skills, delving into techniques such as scat singing and mastering vocal control, drawing inspiration from iconic figures like Ella Fitzgerald and Nina Simone. As she geared up for her debut recital, where she was set to perform alongside a live quartet at one of Seattle's prestigious jazz clubs, excitement filled the air. Weekends were spent immersing ourselves in preparations, fine-tuning her stage presence and wardrobe choices, reminiscent of the joyous times we shared during her ballet lessons before our relocation. It felt like a fleeting moment of respite, a chance to finally exhale amidst the flurry of activities and challenges.

Approximately four weeks following my accident, mere days before Chandler's eagerly anticipated recital, the stormy winds started blowing. "Mom, I am not feeling good," Chandler trembled in a soft voice, catching me off guard. Hoping it was a passing stomach bug or food-related, my mind immediately fretted over the prospect of taking more time off work. It was a haunting Wednesday that etched itself into my memory. I opted to stay home with her, witnessing her unrelenting retching and vomiting throughout the day. Despite initial misgivings, a creeping sense of unease nudged me towards the realization that something more serious may be at play. Urged by intuition, I promptly whisked her to the doctor, who swiftly diagnosed her, "I suspect it is her appendix. She must be rushed to the hospital without delay." With urgency, I arranged for a sitter to watch Cammy, before dashing off to the hospital.

As Chandler's pain escalated, she was administered morphine to help her cope. I stood vigil, a silent witness to every probing test, anxiously awaiting the verdict. The deep-seated fear reflected in her eyes as she timidly questioned me, "Mommy, am I going to die?" I reassured her "No baby, I am right here, and that is not going to happen." But I grappled with a sense of powerlessness in the face of such tumultuous events.

They performed an emergency appendectomy at 11:00 pm. Despite the unwavering support from Marvin and Chandler's father over constant phone calls, I found myself isolated, without the comforting presence of close friends or family. Alone with my thoughts, thousands of miles between me and family, unable to talk to my mom, and asking myself, "Ok superwoman, what do you do now?" I dropped my head and prayed.

Following successful surgery, Chandler's concerns now centered on missing her much-anticipated recital. For the second time in as many weeks, I extended my leave from work to prioritize my family. Presenting her with a pivotal choice, I asked whether she wished to cancel or go through with the recital. Without hesitation, she chose to perform. The show must go on. So, on a school night, five days after surgery, before her classmates, my colleagues, her sister, and Marvin, she sat on a stool, took command of the stage, and sang Etta Jame's iconic song, "At Last." Her metaphorical Supergirl cape was on. I felt a profound sense of pride, akin to what Etta herself might have felt.

As the sixty days bridging my accident and Chandler's appendectomy passed, a familiar longing for the comfort of my East Coast roots crept into my thoughts. Yet, revealing any hint of vulnerability in that moment would have been incongruent with the "I have it all under control" image I portrayed. Subconsciously, I suppressed my anxiety, refusing to reveal my insecurities to anyone, not even my girls. I thought it would make me appear weak. The weight of stress and its toll on my mental and physical well-being steadily compounded as I fought against the challenges.

This inner conflict mirrors the dilemma encountered by many women of color holding positions of leadership. In the realm of coaching engagements, I often find myself fielding queries from managers about assisting black women in embracing vulnerability. It sparks a shared chuckle with my clients, for our instinctive response has always been that disclosing our vulnerabilities may not always find a receptive or safe space. However, my transformative experiences in Seattle have prompted a reevaluation of the concept. I now contemplate how being willing to open about one's frailties can foster relatability and cultivate emotional well-being.

 ## Golden Egg

Vulnerability refers to being open about your limitations, emotional risks, or imperfections without self-criticism. It precedes resiliency. Being vulnerable is a form of self-care. It can make you stronger, reduce your stress and provide the base layer for resiliency. Just be mindful of who and how you share your vulnerable side with. Not only will you be a better leader, most of all you will be better for yourself and your loved ones.

Storm 3

My youngest daughter, Camdyn, affectionately known as Cammy, has dyslexia. When we relocated, finding a suitable school for her proved to be challenging. Fortunately, my relocation package included a school consultant tasked with aiding us in identifying the right educational institution. Unlike the number of options in our former community, Seattle offered only one school that catered to her unique learning requirements—Hamlin Robinson. Navigating the intricacies of developing an Individualized Education Program (IEP) was hard, exacerbated by the fact that I was a single mother in a new city, amplifying my sense of inadequacy and jumbled priorities. Despite these pressures, I stoically persisted, buoyed by the mantra of 'Never let them see you sweat!'

Cammy encountered difficulties adapting to the new learning methodology embraced by the school. It was evident that she found it ineffective. With limited alternatives at hand, I redirected my focus towards fostering joy in other facets of her life. Bonding over activities she enjoyed sharing with me, such as getting our hair and nails done to mitigate her stress.

As anticipated, another hurdle loomed on the horizon, following the pattern of challenges coming in threes. It struck precisely thirty days later, on a Saturday afternoon as the three of us were at the hair salon. Engaged in a timeless tradition handed down from black mothers to their daughters, we immersed ourselves in the quintessential experience of spending hours at the beauty salon awaiting our turn. The best hairstylists had a long list of clients who always came on Saturday. The scenario was familiar—scheduled for a 10:00am appointment only to endure prolonged waits, interspersed with dashes for lunch and impromptu homework sessions while sipping my special "coffee" that may have concealed a splash of bourbon to maintain my composure.

Amidst this routine, we would get tidbits of local gossip, ranging from personal affairs to community news, a drive-by of car trunk contraband, all while hoping to be lucky and leave by 5:00pm. This ritual is one of the fondest memories I have with my mom, and I smiled as I shared it with the girls.

Cammy stood up after getting her French Press hairdo, her hair sleek and shiny as she shook it out. She felt all grown up with her hair down, and I loved seeing her smile and feel beautiful. We were getting ready to leave for dinner together when suddenly, her knees buckled, and she lurched forward. It happened quickly but looked strange. I asked if she'd felt that before, and she said yes, a few times. I was immediately racked with guilt for not noticing. Wondering how I missed something so obvious.

We went back to her doctor, who said she needed more tests. So, thirty days after Chandler's surgery and sixty days after my fall, I was back in the hospital with Cammy. She stayed overnight for an electroencephalogram to check her brain waves. The results showed she had atonic seizures—Cammy had epilepsy. She had to start medication, which meant more time in the hospital to monitor the dosage and any side effects.

Fortunately, Cammy eventually outgrew the seizures and no longer needed medication. The anxiety from our challenges in Seattle lingered for years until I realized the value of being vulnerable and seeking support. This marked the point where my resilience surfaced, allowing me to lead by example.

Life is not a dress rehearsal where you get to retake the same scene. You make decisions and adjustments, learning from each experience. Although these were very hard and painful moments in my life, I learned to ask for help, advocate for myself.

During this time, I should have confided in someone about everything that was going on. The only person at work who knew the full story was my assistant, Evelyn. She often stepped in to help with tasks like picking up the kids or groceries, always supportive and wanting me to succeed. Understanding the challenges faced by (Black) women in such roles, she had my back.

I also should have asked for a short leave to manage my life. However, being in the position for less than a year made me hesitant to do so. I kept pushing myself to juggle it all, a common pattern of prioritizing others over oneself.

I do not regret my choices. I have given myself grace and learned to grow and manage life more effectively. You can do this by asking yourself how many times you find yourself pushing through, prioritizing everything and everyone over your needs. Take a moment to write your personal resilience story and reflect on what you could do differently.

Hope and Resiliency

I am fond of saying, "Life is what happens between the things you plan." Life is unpredictable. I never planned to be a single parent or move across the country from my base of family and friends. I did not plan for my mom to be ill or have multiple crises to navigate. But I did believe I could manage through anything that came my way.

During difficult times are you able to see the bright side of things? Mindset has everything to do with moving forward after hardships. I considered myself a true optimist. Some of this I credit my parents for demonstrating positivity and joy through hardships when I was child. Although I did not fully grasp the value of positive thinking until later, I believe it is a key factor in my ability to rebound. Resilience, I've come to learn, is fundamental to maintaining overall well-being and contentment, and being able to move forward after the storms.

As you successfully recover from tough situations, pay attention to what you did well that helped you find solutions. These steps are often repeatable and can help build your confidence and fortify your ability to conquer whatever comes next. I made it through my perfect storms. Little did I realize this was a harbinger preparing me for even greater challenges ahead.

If you are dealing with multiple challenges and feeling lost, remember that resilience can be nurtured, and you can change and influence your outcomes. Here are a few additional strategies to support you on this journey.

 ## Golden Eggs

1. Being strong does not mean doing it all or doing it all by yourself. You do not need to be all things to all people.
2. Learn to be vulnerable. Ask for help. It makes you more relatable.
3. Always focus on the positives in your life.
4. Forgiveness. My pastor once told me, "Forgiveness is not about forgetting, but remembering things differently." Forgive yourself and others. Stop judging and let go of the things that do not serve you.

Maturity is a magical thing, now you see it, now you don't. You are always maturing and evolving. You never stop growing, that is the magic of life. You have time to learn resiliency if you just be still...

6
REINVENTION

"Life is a canvas; you are the artist. Envision the masterpiece you can create. You, the artist, armed with a set of brushes and paints that are uniquely yours. Your palette holds a rich array of colors and shades, each one a representation of your life experiences, relationships and knowledge. And now, you are on the verge of painting your life anew." I used this vivid analogy in my commencement address to the graduating class of University of New Haven.

The inspiration for this analogy came to me during a trip to the Museum of Modern Art, where I visited Claude Monet's magnificent *Water Lilies* triptych. Awed by the intricate beauty of his water lily garden in Giverny, I learned that Monet painted this iconic series over the final three decades of his life. Renowned for his tireless work ethic, often spending long stretches of up to fourteen hours a day at his easel, Monet would review his daily progress. If dissatisfied with any aspect, he fearlessly painted over it. In Monet's artistic philosophy, there existed no mistakes—only opportunities to reinvent, reshape, and reimagine his creations.

Life is the stuff that happens to you in-between the plans you make. As the saying goes, "Life be lifeing," the oft used

internet quote describing situations of extraordinary challenges amidst the ordinariness of life. Plato stated that
necessity is the mother of invention. My twist on this old
proverb is, "Necessity is the mother of reinvention." The
need to pivot, renew, or reinvent is often spurred by life's
milestones, unplanned events, or life-changing experiences. These instances serve as catalysts for you to embrace
change, adapt, and begin a journey of reimagining your life.

Life milestones such as graduations, marriage, starting
a family, significant birthdays, or retirement, are natural
checkpoints that might prompt you to reflect on your current path and decide to shift. However, it is often something
formidable like job loss, divorce, loss of a loved one, health
crises and similar hurdles that force you to change out of
necessity. As with any change, the first foray into reimagining
your life can be paralyzing. Whether you are being proactive, or responding to a challenging event or circumstances,
there are basic steps you can take towards reinventing and
launching a new phase of your life.

Discover inspiration through these three compelling
stories centered on resiliency, reinvention and renewal. In
the first narrative, I vulnerably continue sharing my journey of resilience and how it empowered me to reset and
reinvent my life following a job loss. You will also meet two
extraordinary individuals I deeply admire, Derek Phillips
and Dr. Charlotte Jones-Burton. Derek shares his story of
moving from a truant, at risk youth, to an inspirational leader
committed to empowering Black men. Nephrologist and
biopharma executive, Dr. Charlotte Jones-Burton shows how
commitment to her vision of equity in healthcare helped her
pivot from practicing medicine to an executive and influ-
encer creating better health outcomes for Black and Brown
communities. Their stories illuminate how they navigated

change to further advance their lifelong visions and commitments, offering you valuable insights for your own journey of transformation and empowerment.

From VP of Global Diversity to The Strategy Chick, Self-empowerment Artist

"You will have a successful career, it just won't be here," remarked the Chief Human Resource Officer as I entered her office for what I thought was to be my annual review. Instead, I was let go. I felt ambushed, her words cut through me like knives, leaving me struggling to breath. "Et tu, Brutus?," I whispered inwardly, feeling the betrayal like what Julius Caesar must have felt, I slowly turned, confronting my own tribunal of 'traitors' gathered to deliver the fatal blow. Among them were my manager of a mere five months, a corporate attorney and the head of HR, the latter's attempted hug feeling more like a dagger in my heart. My immediate concern was for Chandler and Cammy–'Oh my God, my girls, my girls, my girls.'

In the aftermath of the previous tumultuous year of perfect storms, I could not fathom being unemployed or relocating once more. I could only think about how this was going to impact them as I absorbed what was happening. I resorted to deep breaths and subtly touching my finger to my nose–an old trick used to hold back tears. I stood there, stunned in disbelief but I mustered the strength to definitively tell the HR executive I preferred she did not touch me. In that moment, a hug from her, was the furthest thing from solace I could ever imagine.

I was seated across from them, looking down and observing their blurred reflections dance on the sleek oval maple and rosewood conference table. I was conscious of them talking but my mind shut off, as if to protect me from further hurt, though, deep down, I longed to curse them out. I listened as my manager of five months, a Black man, explained why he was pushing me out of my job. When it was all done, I exited the office without glancing back, never laying eyes on them again. Heading to my office, I grabbed my coat and walked out to the parking garage where the chilling Seattle mist and gray skies mirrored the feeling of my spirit. Finally settling in my car, I slumped into my seat, called Marvin, and let the pent-up anguish, anger and raw emotion of the past two years leave my body in a gut-wrenching scream.

The Aftermath

I really had no time to think about myself, my primary concern was my family. So, I did what I do best, put on my superwoman cape and put everyone else first. This did not only happen to me, but it also happened to our family. We were just beginning to feel like Seattle was home. Have you relocated for your career? Moving a family takes more time to settle and establish a new community. I have clients tell me it takes at least two years before the dust settles.

Marvin and I had just married that August. A blended family of five kids who had all suffered significant trauma and times of instability. My sons, Fred, Malcom, and Paul, needed my support having lost their mom to cancer and my girls lived through my divorce and relocation away from their dad. These factors weighed heavily as I told them what happened and that we were moving back east. Chandler was a high school freshman in the top performing arts school in Seattle. She loved her school and did not want to leave. I knew Cammy would be better off but getting resettled would prove to be challenging. In hindsight, I should have focused more on our emotions than the mechanics of processing the move back east.

The Working Mom's Dilemma

Many of you are managing careers and multi-generational homes. When you experience extreme challenges that impact your household, what do you prioritize? How transparent are you in sharing the issues and collaborating on solutions with your family? Here are a few basic tips to help you navigate:

Give yourself some timeout. Acknowledge your emotions and determine what support you need at home or professionally. Evaluate the challenges against your values, purpose and remember your why. Determine if you need to recalibrate anything.

Write down key messages your family needs to know. What is changing and why? How will it impact them? Make sure to tailor your words to the age specific needs of your family.

Set aside time to talk with them without distractions. Create a place of safety for you and your family to be vulnerable and honest. Our kids sense and know more than we realize. Being straightforward demonstrates concern and respect.

Manage expectations, yours and theirs. It is important to ask what their thoughts or needs might be. It is equally as important for you to articulate what you need.

Leave the door open for future conversations. It takes time to process the impact of big changes. Emotions will be triggered at different times. It is important to acknowledge them as part of the healing process.

This occurred in December, so I decided it was best to let the girls complete their school year in Seattle. The ensuing months would be a blur as I sold our Seattle home, moved into temporary housing, enrolled them into new schools in New York, and had the movers pack and transport our things back east. What I did not do was take time to grieve for my loss or think about what was next for my career. The final flight back to New York was eerily like it all began. The three of us, silently anxious for our futures, keeping faith that all would be okay.

The one bright thing we all anticipated was returning to Martha's Vineyard for two weeks. I devoted the summer to family and planned experiences for us to share. The girls were used to going each summer and now we would reconnect with old friends and family, and I could remember the joy of being in my happy place where Marvin and I first met. I needed this time to manage my anxiety over what was next for my career.

Reflection and Recovery

Once the school year was underway, I turned my attention to blending our families, renovating our home, and caring for mom. A full year passed before I could reflect on what happened and what I wanted to do next.

I began with analyzing what I learned from this experience. Starting with my initial conversation with the hiring manager, the romance of the interview process and getting the offer, through on-boarding, building relationships and the breakup. I could see the flaws in the process that did not set me up for success. There were two areas which stood out, they were the absence of leadership development and executive coaching. These would later become the foundation of my purpose and practice as The Strategy Chick®.

My early career with GE provided an opportunity for continuous leadership development. Management courses at their famed Crotonville learning center expanded my range of skills and understanding of the core competencies of good leadership. I should have used this knowledge as a filter before accepting the position in Seattle. It had a dual reporting structure to the heads of corporate communications and human resources. This should have been a red flag that I probed more before accepting the offer. Shortly after starting, I recognized the lack of alignment between these two leaders and how it would affect my success.

I also began seeing inconsistencies in how leaders were treated across key functions. Much about the culture at headquarters felt mercurial, quite different than what I imagined it would be based on the congenial, diverse experiences I was accustomed to in local markets. I also grew more cautious as I learned more about why other senior people of color left the organization after two or three years. In hindsight, I should have spent more time upfront doing my homework and asking about the culture and why they left. Another lesson learned.

As I gained clarity on key stakeholders and relationships, I was finally given the opportunity to receive executive coaching. I excitedly prepared for my first session when I learned the parameters for their coaching model. There was one coach for the entire senior leadership team and their direct reports. To my dismay, I could not select my own coach. Nor could I access the coach directly. Instead, I had to go through the chairman's office to request an appointment and wait for them to provide session details.

Following my coaching certification with International Coach Federation (ICF), I understood why this model was flawed and less than optimal for leadership development. It did little to foster psychological safety and violated ICF coaching guidelines. I vividly remember the moment I realized the coach was not there for my benefit. She did not offer me leadership assessments, conduct 360s or provide feedback on how to leverage my expertise in the existing corporate culture. All tools I now effectively use to support leaders in shaping their organizations, developing talent, and enhancing their impact.

My job loss was the defining moment that helped me create a new vision and purpose for my life. Using the Wheel of Life and a vision board, I assessed several factors impacting my choices, including age, finances, family needs and what I enjoyed doing. I also continued therapy with my doctor to manage my anxiety, anger and insecurities that surface when you are unemployed. I determined it was time to leverage my talent, experience, and passion to coach and teach others to live and work powerfully.

I believe every woman deserves a great coach. Every talented person of color, who earned a seat at the table deserves a great coach and safe place to be vulnerable. I would become that coach, leveraging my life experiences, business, and communication skills to help other women and people of color succeed. I never want another woman or person of color to experience what happened to me or be caught off guard. I am passionately dedicated to sharing tools, wisdom, and strategies, combined with my unique interpersonal style with clients to increase their awareness of how to play the game, and become better leaders. It was time to reinvent myself, to shed my corporate skin and become The Strategy Chick®, self-empowerment artist, executive coach and entrepreneur.

Strategic Steps to Recovery and Rebranding After Trauma

These are suggestions on how to jump start your new journey. They were essential to my metamorphosis. It is important to make daily efforts towards your goal. It will increase your self-empowerment and confidence.

1. Just be still. Allow time to process what happened and grieve.

2. Talk with your loved ones. Friends and family who support and love you.

3. Seek any additional counseling necessary. Therapeutic, spiritual, legal, financial. Determine how much time you can afford to not have a steady income source.

4. Only deal with the necessary things that must be done. Do not make major decisions or hasty changes.

5. Do something that brings you joy.

6. Get creative—make a vision board of your future life.

7. Take inventory of skills, talents, marketable assets. Determine what additional skills or training you might need. Conduct personal research to develop your brand narrative and resources.

8. Write a newspaper article interviewing you a year from now.

9. Construct a new biography, personal marketing page, and resume if needed.

10. Update your social media to reflect the new brand and strategic direction.

11. Remember that you are unique and wonderful, and this too shall pass.

I launched The Strategy Chick® in 2015 following one additional corporate executive position. My practice has grown tremendously, and I know that I am making a difference in the lives of others and helping them step into their power.

Have you experienced a job loss or other career changing event that forced you to re-evaluate why you chose that career path. How did it alter your vision, values, and core beliefs? Or did it make you question why and what you were supposed to learn from the experience? I have assembled a few Golden Eggs of things I wish I had known, based on lessons I learned from my experience. They offer invaluable insights if you are just learning how to navigate the complexities of career transitions at the executive level. You may find them helpful in evaluating your next opportunity.

 ## Golden Eggs

1. **Consult an employment attorney prior to accepting a job offer**. They can assist you in negotiating your terms and include provisions for exit strategies. It is crucial to plan for potential job termination upfront.

2. **Seek insights from past employees.** Before committing to a new role, connect with former employees who held the position and those who have left the company to gain insights into the organizational culture beyond what current leaders may disclose.

3. **Handle dual reporting structures.** Whenever faced with dual reporting structures, align goals with both managers and address any concerns upfront to ensure clarity and avoid potential conflicts.

4. **Share onboarding plan**. Share your onboarding plan with a trusted individual in HR or a senior executive from another organization to ensure you are well-equipped for success in your new role. Also inquire about leadership development and request an executive coach of your choosing.

5. **Build a strong team.** Evaluate your team promptly and assemble competent, loyal advisors. Replace individuals who may harbor resentment for not obtaining your position to maintain a supportive and capable team.

6. **Prioritize and invest time to establish key relationships.** Focus on your important stakeholders and build quality relationships with them.

7. **Consider family needs in detail before relocating.** If relocation is necessary and you have a family, possibly consider working in the new position for at least a year before relocating your entire family. Negotiate relocation expenses upfront to make an informed decision and avoid uprooting your family for a potentially unsuitable role.

Derek Phillips, Founder, Executive Director Real Dads Network

"We are honoring Derek Phillips, who is devoting his
life to making a difference for dads across the country
through his non-profit "Real Dads Network.""
Whit Johnson, Good Morning America,
Father's Day Segment.

Father's Day marked a significant milestone in the life of Derek Phillips, the visionary behind Real Dads Network. In a feature story on Good Morning America, Derek was recognized for his relentless dedication to empowering Black men to become exemplary fathers. Over the past two decades, his nonprofit organization has rallied a diverse group of professionals—from teachers, doctors, lawyers, and financial planners to athletes—to offer crucial support and guidance to black men, encouraging them to elevate themselves and build brighter futures for their families. Driven by the challenges of his upbringing and a heartfelt promise made to his late mother, Derek defied the grim statistics that often-enveloped individuals in similar circumstances. I share his story for inspiration to those who think they cannot overcome the hand they are dealt. Like many of you, Derek was an unsung hero, working tirelessly on a vision to improve life for Black dads. Until one day, he looked up and his vision had become a reality. Never give up on your dreams.

"I could have easily fallen through the cracks. By the time I was in second grade, I was already struggling, facing consequences for skipping school. After my mother's passing, I found myself unwanted by my siblings, deemed 'The Bad Child.' Yet, amidst these adversities, my mother's voice echoed in my mind, urging me to persevere: 'You will finish school, and you will rise above.' I refused to disappoint her."

Hailing from Brooklyn and being the youngest among eight siblings, Derek Phillips bore witness to hardships and tragedies that far exceeded his youthful age. He navigated a world shadowed by alcoholism, illiteracy, and shattered aspirations, yet defying the odds, he became a teacher, role model, and inspiration within his family and community.

At just ten years old, Derek's mother died unexpectedly, leaving no directives or provisions for his care. Amidst the grief of losing his mother, Derek endured profound feelings of abandonment and rejection when his older siblings refused to take him. Almost falling into the hands of the judicial system as a ward of the court, his elder sister agreed to raise him despite grappling with her own battles—nurturing her own children while combating alcoholism. The impact of these experiences ignited Derek's fervent desire to rise above his circumstances and set him towards a mission of lifting others from adversity and assuming the role of a dedicated and nurturing father within his own family.

Appreciative of the help he received, Derek started to turn things around. But without strong role models to guide him, staying on the right track became tough. Eventually, he stopped going to school and ended up back on the streets. Looking back, Derek admits that despite his smarts and dreams of doing better, he just could not find the drive to stay in school. Missing so many days meant he should have repeated 8th grade. However, since New York schools did not hold students back twice, he got pushed into one of Brooklyn's roughest high schools. Things looked bleak until he was introduced to The Nation of Islam.

Immersed in a culture that emphasized racial solidarity, self-empowerment, and discipline, Derek found a nurturing environment that became the foundation for his growth. Being part of a community that consisted of determined, resilient Black men committed to mutual support, self-improvement, and uplifting their families, Derek could see future possibilities and knew that his calling was to empower men of color to be real dads, which became the name of his organization.

Have you ever found yourself in a situation where everything seemed dark, hopeless, and beyond your grasp? It is natural to initially feel like a victim, questioning why things are happening the way they are. So, how can you shift this perspective? It all starts with focusing on yourself to reclaim your sense of balance and empowerment. Take the time to reflect on your core values, dreams, and goals. Stay open to drawing inspiration from unexpected sources and individuals. Derek firmly believes that these steps were pivotal in his own journey towards success and transformation.

While Derek did not officially become a member of the Nation of Islam, he drew invaluable lessons from its emphasis on self-improvement and empowerment, skills that proved instrumental in shaping his life's trajectory. Initially focusing on his own family circle, Derek became a role model for his nieces and nephews, setting a powerful example by leading a clean lifestyle free of alcohol, tobacco, and drugs. His commitment paid off as he went on to complete his high school education, bachelor's and two master's degrees and spearhead the development of acclaimed community initiatives aimed at aiding vulnerable young people.

It Takes a Village

Throughout Derek's journey of self-discovery, relationships remained a critical element in his evolution. Transitioning from being a neglected youth who seldom showed up for classes to someone who secured scholarships for college, he acknowledges the profound impact of his mentors at SUNY New Paltz. Derek attributes his academic success to his Black history professors, who extended their support beyond the classroom by writing to him during summer recess. These letters not only aimed to enhance his writing and English skills but also served as a catalyst for encouraging Derek to make more mindful decisions and prioritize his long-term aspirations over short-lived immediate gratification.

Mentors, sponsors, and advocates can appear in different forms and at various stages in our personal and professional development. Reflecting on your own key relationships and how you nurture them is essential. Revisit the sphere of influence exercise from earlier chapters and consider how you can further invest in and sustain those connections. Taking proactive steps to strengthen and maintain these relationships can significantly impact your growth and success.

Derek was also fortunate to meet Maria during his college years, who would become not just his wife but his lifelong best friend and support. Together, they raised two remarkable daughters, Jordyn and Maya. This partnership enabled Derek to fulfill his deepest aspirations—to be a devoted and involved father, a role model vastly different from his own absent father figure. Derek found in his family a source of fulfillment and purpose, inspiring him to strive for the kind of paternal presence he missed in his childhood.

In 2019, Derek retired from his teaching career as an Assistant Principal in the New Your City School System, to dedicate himself entirely to expanding his organization. His unwavering commitment remains centered on fostering self-empowerment through education. With a clear vision in mind, Derek aims to establish fatherhood and family centers that serve as pillars of support, aiming to fortify the structure of Black families and communities by empowering fathers.

His mission is to create spaces that not only offer resources and guidance but also instill a sense of strength and unity within families, envisioning a future where paternal presence plays a vital role in shaping resilient and thriving communities.

Derek's transformation did not happen overnight. Through the power of relationships and resiliency, he created a vision and reshaped his life. When it was time to retire, he could devote his time to expanding on his vision to uplift and support Black men. I asked Derek to share a few success tips to help someone trying to find a purpose and re-imagine their lives.

1. Self-empowerment starts with passion. Find something you truly care about. Then you will commit to the hard work.
2. If you have not found your passion, don't worry. Talk to people. Engage in conversation. Listen and learn.
3. Expose yourself to different events and communities.
4. Step out of your comfort zone.
5. Start with the end in mind and plan backwards.
6. Shift to a growth mindset. Failing is part of growth. Missing the goal is not a mistake, it is learning. Everyone falls, it is part of the process.
7. Give hope to others, it will come back to you.

Dr. Charlotte Jones-Burton

"Becoming a doctor was not a choice,
it was an expectation..."
Dr. Charlotte Jones-Burton, Partner 2Flo Ventures,
Board Member and Biopharmaceutical Executive

Charlotte epitomizes what it means to lead a purpose-driven life. As a physician who has witnessed, experienced, and researched systematic racism within healthcare, Charlotte is dedicated to a mission of advancing health equity and her actions have led to transforming an industry. She had the foresight to see that being a successful nephrologist would not be enough to have a significant impact. So, Charlotte made the bold decision to transition from practicing medicine to becoming a biopharmaceutical executive. While treating patients and saving lives was undoubtedly noble, her purpose transcended individual care. Charlotte was resolute –her purpose would be addressing the health inequities that disproportionately affect black and brown communities.

Early childhood experiences shaped Charlotte's career choices and laid the foundation for her vision of bringing healthcare to black and brown communities. Raised as an only child of a single working mother, Charlotte spent significant time with her maternal grandmother who suffered from diabetes. "She relied on me to administer her insulin and other medications. In essence I became her eyes and her feet as diabetes damaged her nerves. I only had to look around me to see how so many relatives and neighbors had little access to healthcare or medicine." Charlotte shared how this became a constant source of motivation through all the challenges she faced becoming a doctor.

"My mom set the expectation that I would be a doctor. She kept a sign on the wall which read, 'I know I am somebody, because God didn't make no junk.' She taught me the power of positive affirmation which still resonates with me today."

Charlotte articulated a clear vision for the impact she wanted to have in healthcare. Upon completing her medical and master's degrees and training (residency, fellowship) in Baltimore, MD., Charlotte quickly recognized the limitations in academic medicine and the politics involved in access to healthcare. She knew practicing medicine would not be enough to create the level of change needed in underserved communities. She was not sure how she was going to push her agenda forward until the day a recruiter called.

The Pivot

A chance call from an executive recruiter introduced Charlotte to the business side of medicine. She realized becoming an executive in biopharma with a medical degree would place her in rooms where key decisions and funding were made. She aspired to own her seat at the table.

Charlotte not only made the pivot to corporate, but she also made strategic career moves to develop targeted medicines for fighting kidney disease, keeping her focused on her purpose. As Charlotte shifted from practicing medicine to being a corporate leader, she widened her circle of advisors to target her growth areas. This included increasing exposure to board level executives, developing policy and providing strategic guidance to the executive team on a billion-dollar business acquisition. I became one of her trusted advisors, honing and expanding her leadership impact.

Although Charlotte was adept at leading highly skilled teams of professionals performing medical procedures, navigating a corporate culture presents a different set of challenges. In medical teams, roles and expectations are clearly defined; everyone knows their responsibilities and who is in charge. When they step into the operating room, they are fully prepared, with no room for second-guessing a leading surgeon when a patient's life is at stake. In stark contrast, corporate team meetings often involve ambiguity and a lack of clear direction, where decisions are made amid microaggressions and biases that can challenge diverse leaders. Charlotte faced these hurdles head-on. To enhance her leadership impact across the various levels of stakeholders she engages with, she effectively leverages executive coaching.

Throughout her transition from practicing medicine to serving on corporate boards, Charlotte remained steadfast in her vision for health equity in black and brown communities. She attributes this to having a clear and concise vision, along with the ability to effectively communicate and engage others, even as she navigated personal changes. If you find yourself facing similar challenges, needing to pivot, or seeking reinvention, remember your "why." This guiding principle can sustain you through your own transformation.

It's All About the Relationships

There can never be enough emphasis placed on the power of relationships. I asked Charlotte to share thoughts on this topic. "I believe in it so much so that I founded an entire organization based on that principle. Working individually, we might get recognized for our contributions. But working together we can have the impact to drive sustainable change."

Charlotte believes in the importance of relationships and harnessing the collective power of women. Committed to her mission, she utilized this strength to establish Women of Color in Pharma (WOCIP) with the goal of promoting health equity. The organization's focus on self-actualization and self-investment aligns with my fundamental belief in self-empowerment, which includes elements such as self-reflection, confronting anxieties, and mastering effective communication.

Within WOCIP, women are provided with a supportive and uplifting space that encourages them to challenge traditional thought patterns, embark on journeys of self-discovery, and engage in mutual celebration of other women. These are all critical to help them achieve influence and power to contribute to altering the health outcomes of marginalized populations.

How have your relationships nurtured and helped you to grow? What things are you doing to show appreciation or develop others? The process of developing resiliency and reinventing yourself relies on your connections with others. Neuropsychologist, Dr. Richard Boyatzis, underscores the importance of relationships in his intentional change theory. They are at the center of his model on the process of self-discovery and change. The more you engage others in your vision, the more likely you are to achieve it.

What are some of the ways you have supported friends during change or difficult periods in their lives? In times of adversity, supporting friends facing challenges can be a profound and impactful gesture. It is essential to reflect on your strengths and unique resources, approaching the situation with creativity and empathy to provide meaningful support.

This approach aligns with the profound wisdom shared by Kahlil Gibran in his renowned work, The Prophet. His timeless words convey a deeper truth about the essence of giving: true generosity lies not in material offerings but in the genuine giving of oneself. By embodying this principle and offering authentic support, we can make a lasting impact on the lives of those around us, enriching both their journey and our own. Charlotte embodies this in everything she does.

I admire and respect Charlotte's accomplishments. But it is her unwavering support as a friend that places her atop the list of women I admire. During the COVID pandemic, I was diagnosed with Chronic Myeloid Leukemia (CML). A silent killer that, left untreated, would slowly take my life. As a Black woman, the stark reality of dying early struck me hard in that moment. I needed to educate myself on the best drugs and treatment for me. Through my work with Charlotte and WOCIP, I knew the importance of diversity in clinical trials. Charlotte leveraged her clinical expertise and knowledge to help me evaluate my care as a patient, while balancing her love for me as a friend.

Charlotte's impact continues to grow as she persistently seeks new pathways and partnerships to support her vision of equitable access and improved health outcomes. Today, WOCIP boasts a network of over 4,000 dedicated members and followers committed to driving change and enhancing their self-empowerment. She remains focused on securing funding for the development of drugs that could potentially eradicate diseases such as kidney failure and sepsis, which disproportionately affect our communities.

These are incredible contributions from that young girl raised by a single mom in Arkansas, California, and Ohio. Who became a woman, whose destiny was preordained.

I asked her one final question, "What can you say about resilience and reinvention?"

"Some people believe you are born resilient. I do not. I believe you can create your own resiliency through the power of vision and relationships. When I was young, my dolls were my collective. I talked to them, sharing my deepest secrets. As I got older, I knew I needed my tribe to get through life. I lean on relationships. This is the North Star for WOCIP.

Charlotte also shared a few comments for my Golden Eggs. In her words, here are three things she knows for sure:

1. My steps have been ordered. I do not second guess. I just pay attention and am ready when the call comes.
2. Self-love, confidence, and care are essentials to my success.
3. As the African proverb says, "If you want to go fast, go alone; if you want to go far, go together."

Summary

Whether you are totally reinventing yourself as I did after my job loss, or making smaller pivots as Derek and Charlotte did, having a strong vision will help you remain focused. Investing in others and nurturing your relationships will help you engage them and assist you in remaining committed during times of change. Unlocking your power is in your hands. The simple strategies shared in each story are tools to help you plant the seeds for personal growth so you can bloom in your own season.

CONCLUSION

I am grateful for the opportunity to share these personal and professional stories, intertwined with coaching strategies designed to inspire and guide you towards unlocking your personal power. While each narrative is unique, they all underscore the importance of cultivating a foundation of self-empowerment. The ability to reflect on your past, face your fears, and effectively communicate lays the groundwork for fostering a growth mindset.

Reflection serves as a powerful tool for self-evaluation. Utilize it to define your values and craft a vision for your future. You may find you need to recalibrate and that is perfectly acceptable. For women of color, the road towards self-empowerment is strewn with hurdles. Extending grace to yourself and allowing room for self-renewal are crucial for your well-being.

Consider the example of Simone Biles, who made the difficult decision to step back during the Tokyo Olympics. Despite facing criticism and grappling with self-doubt, she prioritized her well-being. It required courage, yet she granted herself the time to heal and made a triumphant return two years later as the greatest gymnast of all times.

Though subtle, microaggressions possess the potential to undermine your personal power. Building a supportive network of allies and confidants with whom you can share your experiences is instrumental in gaining perspective and countering negative self-talk.

Establishing a network of strong relationships is also essential to building your confidence and power. These connections are a source of validation and support as you navigate through periods of uncertainty. With these fundamental components in place, you will discover greater resilience and the capacity to continuously reinvent yourself over time.

Many inquire about my ability to maintain a positive and joyful outlook despite facing numerous challenges. While I do attribute this to my optimism, I recognize that not everyone finds it easy to locate the silver lining. In such instances, coaching can prove invaluable in helping you create strategies to move your life forward. The exercises outlined in the book are thoughtfully crafted to guide you through a journey of introspection, assessment, and communication skills—all aimed at empowering you to own your narrative.

As I pen down this book, we find ourselves amidst one of the most dynamic periods for women of color in the annals of the United States. Women of color are making bold moves and finding inspiration from women who are using their power like Former First Lady Michelle Obama or Former Vice President Kamala Harris. Although these women are internationally known, there are women like you and like me, who are making a difference in our communities by empowering others. Black women are the fastest growing group of entrepreneurs in the U.S. This is the energy needed to show that women of color will no longer be relegated to menial jobs and less pay.

Women from diverse backgrounds and racial identities are using their collective power to shift mindsets and create opportunities to bloom. A master gardener knows that each flower contributes to the beauty of the garden and blooms at different times.

To fully embrace this moment here are three things you can do to leverage the energy and expand your own power base.

1. Step out of your comfort zone, pick a cause you are passionate about and join a multigenerational team in your community. Sharing your talents with an organization that has a need will uplift and validate you.
2. Reverse mentoring. Mentoring is positioned as someone senior and more experienced passing advice and wisdom to younger people. Seek to learn from someone younger than you. It helps you stay on the forefront of change.
3. Imagine you are being featured in a New York Times article and draft the story. Why is the paper featuring you? What is your narrative? What key messages do you want the reader to take away from the article?

In my imagined interview with Oprah, when she asks, "What do you know for sure?" I reply, "I know there's a strategy for everything, and that personal power starts with facing yourself. It's the foundation for embracing change and resilience. You can't move forward while looking in the rearview mirror–don't let your past define you. Everyday people are doing extraordinary things. Let their stories inspire you and trust in your own power to live your best life. It's time to *Bloom!*"

REVIEW INQUIRY

Hey, it's Cecilia.

I hope you've enjoyed the book, finding it both useful and fun. I have a favor to ask you.

Would you consider giving it a rating wherever you bought the book? Online book stores are more likely to promote a book when they feel good about its content, and reader reviews are a great barometer for a book's quality.

So please go to the website of wherever you bought the book, search for my name and the book title, and leave a review. If able, perhaps consider adding a picture of you holding the book. That increases the likelihood your review will be accepted!

Many thanks in advance,
Cecilia Carter

WILL YOU SHARE THE LOVE?

Get this book for a friend, associate, or family member!

If you have found this book valuable and know others who would find it useful, consider buying them a copy as a gift. Special bulk discounts are available if you would like your whole team or organization to benefit from reading this. Just visit my website, www.thestrategychick.com.

WOULD YOU LIKE CECILIA CARTER TO SPEAK TO YOUR ORGANIZATION?

Book Cecilia Now!

Cecilia Carter accepts a limited number of speaking/ coaching/training engagements each year. To learn how you can bring her message to your organization visit www.thestrategychick.com.

ACKNOWLEDGMENTS

I did not wake up like this! My journey toward self-empowerment and creation of this book has spanned over 60 years, encompassing six careers, nine companies, fifteen jobs, five relocations, two cross-country moves, alopecia, two marriages, five children, and a battle with cancer. I've experienced both exhilarating highs, and what I perceived were crushing lows. Nurturing *Bloom!* into existence has been a cathartic experience, allowing me the time to reflect on and rejoice in the countless wonderful moments and individuals who have shaped this journey. Through it all, I have been profoundly grateful for the love and support of many.

To Marvin: my blessing. Simply calling you my husband, partner, spouse, best friend, lover and all those other adjectives barely scratches the surface. You are my everything–the one who makes my wildest dreams come true. By the divine forces of God, we were brought together, united by the belief that love can blossom even from the darkest depths of despair, restoring a light that deserves to shine in both our lives. I am a better person because of you. Our love story could be the subject of my next book, but for now, the answer is Love Ballad...

To My Family: Mom, you are with me always and I miss you every single day. I felt your hands guiding mine as I wrote, reminding me I've had the power all along. Dad, thank you for instilling in me the importance of vision and values. Thank you for being a "Real Dad" ready with tough

love while lifting me up, encouraging me to pursue anything I set my mind to. For always being there when my
eyes sought the familiar face in the crowd affirming the
little girl who grew into the woman I am today. Chris, you
will always be smarter than me, but you are still the baby!
I admire how you show up for the family and carry mom's
legacy with tenacity, always putting others first. Cyndi, a
real survivor, I am proud of the love we have built and the
families we've nurtured. You are a role model for me and
many others—thank you for believing I could do this!

Aunt Cleo and Aunt Tootie, together with mom, you
showed me what it means to believe in yourself, to always
lift others and I know the three of you are up there cheering me on. As you would always say, "You fill me so full." To
my cousins Mike and Don Wilbon and Kenny Clark, from
coming of age in the hot summer days, to owning the halls
of Northwestern, I love you like brothers. You each have a
special part of my memories, and it is up to us to carry the
legacy. Joann, my godmother, friend, and surrogate mom,
I do not know where I would be without you. In your voice,
I still hear mom every time. Momma Anita, I love you and
thank you for Marvin. To my Campbell family, like Marvin,
you are my prayers answered. To Chandler and Cammy, I've
poured the best of our ancestors into you both. You are my
greatest love and joy, inspiring me to keep going every day.
To my bonus men, Fred, Malcolm, and Paul, thank you for
allowing me to be your friend, and love you like a mom. Your
acceptance played a crucial role in helping me become the
woman I am today. Lastly, to Caitlin, my daughter-in-love,
and Julian, my grandson, you make our family complete
and give me the honor of being GiGi.

To My Friends: As Gibran wrote in *"The Prophet,"* "Let
your best be for your friends." I am grateful for the friends

from different eras in my life who keep me grounded and remind me to cherish every moment on this Earth. My Snowmosa Crew: Sylvia and Luis, Stephanie and Carl, Doug and Jennienne, Ria and Derek, Laurie and Jeff–thank you for letting my CeCe-isms come to life, and for accepting and loving me unconditionally.

To my sister Dr. Linda Green and all the Brownies, thank you for sharing and entrusting Marvin and Mary's legacy with the girls and me. My dear travel sisters, Dana Fox, Becky Flanigan, and Eire Stewart, thanks for pushing me out of my comfort zone to the caves of Vietnam and the sands of the Sahara, planting fertile ground for me to blossom.

To my childhood friends, Cynthia Scott, Kim Metcalf (in spirit), Warren Kurtz, my third grade Jewish protector who walked me home from school every day in Euclid, and Debbie Prince, whose parents kept us straight and made sure we were home before the streetlights came on! To Dr. Susan Stephens, Rev. Derrick Harkins, Kathy Ko-Chin, and Myra Evans Lapeyrolerie, my ride-or-die "soul" survivors from prep-school escapades to totally badass leaders–each of you have left an indelible mark on my spirit, reminding me to treat each day as the gift it truly is.

To Dana Davis Mitchell, who coined the phrase, "CeCe knows"; there is no one, kinder, sweeter, or more selfless. If I could clone your heart, love would fill the world. To Rachel and Kamal, our "kids" next door, you are my fountain of youth; with you I'll always stay social media savvy and ready to *Bloom!* To my New York lifers–Darryk Floyd, from the times I had hair until the time I didn't, you kept me looking fierce and only my hairdresser knew for sure... love you! Angela Brock-Kyle and Sandy Johnson Harris, you know the backstory behind the stories but loved me, nonetheless. Your encouragement to be true to myself echoes in my ears daily.

I can't leave out my Seattle crew, powerful women I leaned on during my Seattle days. Evelyn Berry, Dana Frank, Carmen Gayton, Wanda Herndon, Gwen Houston, and Princess Ayers-Stewart, thank you for helping me stay resilient and navigate some of my darkest moments. And lastly, my Sorors Janyth and Marilyn, who know where all the bones are buried—you understood my need for growth and sent me off to New York in 1985 with the song, "That's What Friends Are For." I'm still smiling.

My A-Team: I am fortunate to have many people I rely on for spiritual guidance, physical strength and emotional wellbeing. You are my A-Team. Rev. Calvin Butts, your guidance continues to inspire me. I miss our talks, but I feel your spirit and know you are always with me. Dr. Henry McCurtis, your unique blend of talk therapy and scripture helps me navigate every challenge I face. Jimmy Locust, you help me choreograph a fresh start to life as a 48-year-old single mom, by encouraging me to dance my first recital. I still dance like nobody's watching. Andrew Abt, thank you for taking my fitness levels to new heights. Because of you I've gone from a savage mom to embracing my sexy sixties, and I'm not done yet! Tekoa Hash, always by my side for every major life event, and supporting my girls. Along with Latisha, you both always make me feel beautiful inside and out, supporting everything I do.

My Advocates and Sponsors: Each career move introduced me to many incredible people who supported my journey. Among them are a few special individuals who shaped my formative years and cheered me on to reach beyond what I thought was possible. Joe and Myrtle Nunn, you raised me, from "crayons to perfume" as the song

"To Sir With Love" goes. Mary Barneby, when you selected me to deliver the commencement address at University of New Haven and serve on their board, you set the stage for me to seek new ways to inspire others.

Ann Fudge, you encouraged me to start my own business when I was between jobs. You recognized my potential long before I did, and when I finally stopped fighting myself, it marked the beginning of reimagining my possibilities. Jonathan Kirschner, you were invaluable as I transitioned from corporate executive to The Strategy Chick®, and you continue to be one of my strongest advocates.

Kendelle Argrette, you were the first and only client to meet in my home office. Your commitment to showing up and doing the work kept me focused and your faith still helps me move mountains. Adrienne Lotson, thank you for reaching out and forming a friendship when Marvin came into my life. Amy Kavanaugh Mason, you span many categories including my friend group. Our relationship encompasses all of them. As part of my village, you supported Chandler and kept her safe when I could not be there. You have also been my fierce advocate, believing in lifting women where they belong. You brought me into C-suites and boardrooms where I could be seen and blossom.

Paula Boggs, you were a constant light of encouragement during my tenure at Starbucks. Representation matters and seeing your face in board meetings was the first time I did not feel like the "only." Now I am eagerly waiting to read your book.

My Book Team: My family and friends help me live my best life, but it was my book team that held me accountable for bringing my story to the page. It all began when I watched my friend Ruth Rathblott promote *Unhide and Seek*, her inspiring story of learning to embrace her limb difference. I was so encouraged that I asked her to be an accountability partner. Instead, she introduced me to Cathy Fyock, a book coach and award-winning author. How fitting it is for a coach to hire a coach! That partnership led to connecting with Everett O'Keefe and the team at Ignite Press who partnered with my brand gurus Hamilton Brown and Christopher Hayes to make *Bloom!* a reality. I extend my gratitude to my editorial review board—Deb Berman, Cathy Fryock, Rachel Grey, Yvette Walker-Jones, Amy Kavanaugh Mason, and Candace Matthews—and a special nod to Corey duBrowa, one cool dude who I'm blessed to have in my corner.

At the heart of *Bloom!* are the rich stories of everyday people doing extraordinary things. I am grateful to my clients and friends who agreed to share their stories. Louise, I could not make it all work without you. Derek, you are uplifting entire communities one dad at a time, proving that men can blossom too! Kathy, I am certain readers will appreciate the courage it took for you to face yourself and become a more authentic leader. Thank you for being an integral part of my journey.

Charlotte, Delvin, and the women of WOCIP, our relationship has been nurturing and transformative. Delivering the keynote speech at the national conference to over three hundred women of color was a defining moment for me. It served as a catalyst for my commitment to share my voice and empower others on a larger scale. This is just the beginning. We know the struggle is real and there is much work to do. To health equity and beyond, I can't think of better people to stand with in solidarity.

I know I stand on the shoulders of many and would not be where I am today without them. While I cannot mention everyone by name, I am reminded that to whom much is given, much is required. The seeds have been planted, and it's my season to pay it forward. Thanks to all of you, my garden is bountiful and ready to share, helping others to *Bloom!*

ABOUT THE AUTHOR

Cecilia Carter is a renowned self-empowerment artist committed to helping people unlock their power to bring their best and boldest selves to everything they do. Known as The Strategy Chick®, Cecilia combines her intuitive, visionary coaching style with communications experience to create safe spaces for clients to explore and grow. She launched her practice following an expansive career in corporate affairs serving in a broad range of strategic leadership positions for several world class brands. Her experience across top industry sectors makes her highly sought after as a trusted advisor to senior leaders.

Inspirational and compassionate, Cecilia is a frequent speaker and coach supporting thousands of women in their journey of self-empowerment to overcome roadblocks, find their power and bloom.

Cecilia's influential presence has been recognized by Black Enterprise, Fast Company, and Savoy Magazine, ranking her among the top 100 influential African-American women in corporate America. With her exceptional track record and dedication, Cecilia continues to leave an indelible mark in her field.

Cecilia holds degrees from the Kellogg Graduate School of Management and her bachelor's degree from Northwestern University. A member of the National Speakers Bureau, she is also an International Coach Federation (ICF) certified coach. Cecilia received an honorary Doctorate of Humane Letters from the University of New Haven and served as their Commencement speaker in the 2010 graduation ceremony.

Cecilia is the proud mother of 5 gifted young adults and resides in New Rochelle, NY with her husband Marvin.

Cecilia can be reached at: www.thestrategychick.com